DESTINATION EUROPE

Guide for a period of kitchen training

000099825

LT
Editions Jacques Lanore

UNITED
KINGDOM

© **L.T. EDITIONS J. LANORE**   ISBN 2 86268 223 3 - ISSN 1164 60
131, Rue P. Vaillant-Couturier - 92240 MALAKOFF

Tous droits de traduction, d'adaptation et de reproduction par tous procéd
réservés pour tous pays.
La loi du 11 mars 1957 n'autorisant aux termes des alinéas 2 et 3 de l'artic
41, d'une part, que les « copies ou reproduction strictement réservées à l'usag
privé du copiste et non destinées à une utilisation collective » et, d'autre pa
que les analyses et les courtes citations dans un but d'exemple et d'illustratio
« toute représentation et reproduction intégrale ou partielle, faite sans le conse
tement de l'auteur ou de ses ayants droits ou ayants causes, est illicite » (aliné
1er de l'article 40).
Cette représentation ou reproduction, par quelque procédé que ce soit, cons
tuerait donc une contrefaçon sanctionnée par les articles 425 et suivants du Co
pénal.

— 1 —
in the
UNITED KINGDOM
[UK]

by
Derek C Gladwell, OBE
MA, FHCIMA, FRSA
Emeritus Professor and formerly
Head of the School of Food and
Hospitality Management
Sheffield City Polytechnic

Selecting your placement

What kind of training will suit your needs ?

Leaving your own country to train in Great Britain will be a major step in your career. Before you decide to take this step, you should be clear in your own mind about your objectives.

There are many different types of establishment in Britain in which you can obtain good training - the hotel and restaurant sector is the most common choice, but more specialized sectors, such as hospital catering and staff restaurants, are also available. In most of this booklet we shall use the word ''restaurant'', but please remember that we are using this term to include hotels and the other specialized sectors.

To ensure that you get the training which will be most relevant to your future career, you should decide on your focus of interest :

(1) do you eventually want to become a manager or do you want to hold a senior post in food production and service, such as Head Chef, Section Chef (Chef de Partie) ot Maître d'Hôtel ?

(2) do you prefer to work in a large company owning a chain of establishments or in a small establishment of more individual character ?

What kind of training can Britain offer ?

The various styles of restaurant

You will find wide differences in styles of cooking and in the ways in which restaurants are organized and managed. For example, cooking may be ;

classical ''haute cuisine'' which uses Continental methods ;
''home-made'' style, which uses simple cooking methods but can produce meals of very good quality ;

"popular" style, which aims at uniformity and consistency (sometimes throughout all the restaurants of a nationwide chain) and tends to use a large proportion of pre-prepared foods ;

"large-scale" style, which is used for hospitals, industrial catering and residential welfare establishments and for which recipes, equipment and food materials are designed to produce good quality meals in very large quantities.

In order to illustrate these differences, some thumbnail sketches of typical sectors may be helpful to you. Please remember, however, that each of these sketches is a generalization and that in reality there is a huge range of restaurants, all uniquely different from one another.

(A) Top grade classical restaurants

There are a small number of restaurants which offer the highest standards of classical cuisine. Typically, they have a relatively high proportion of very skilled staff, are fairly labour-intensive, and charge high prices. They are usually organized on the traditional "partie" system (ie, the kitchen is organized on the basis of a number of specialized sections or "parties", each under a "Chef de Partie"). Many of these restaurants are internationally famous. Some are very profitable, whilst others find it difficult to secure enough revenue to meet their very high level of costs.

(B) Other classical restaurants

A rather larger number of restaurants also seek to use classical methods of cooking and are organized on the partie system, but without aiming at such outstanding quality or charging such high prices. Some are very successful, whilst others find considerable difficulty in consistently producing food of the right quality.

(C) Popular (chain) restaurants

The main feature of this type of restaurant is precision planning of the method of operation. The management researches the market as carefully as possible, then specifies in detail the menu, the standard recipes for each dish, the definition of quality for each foodstuff purchased, the cooking procedures, the most suitable type of equipment for the kitchen, and a system of accurate costing and cash control. From the place in which you train. It can be an advantage, when seeking appointments later in your career, to have worked for a famous chef or manager, or for a renowned hotel or restaurant. A "name" does help ! And, of course, if you work for an international chain of hotels and restaurants, you may find it easier to get a post in yet another overseas country. In this connection, it is worth keeping in mind that the world's most famous hotel group (Hilton) and its largest group (Holiday Inns) are now both owned by British companies.

In short, Britain can offer good training opportunities in all sectors of the industry, but has a different scale of values compared with many of the other countries in Europe. This means that very good opportunities exist outside the field of classical restaurants - and trainees would be well advised to give careful consideration to such opportunities when selecting their training placement in Britain.

Learning the language

Improving your knowledge of English will be one of the most important benefits of your stay.

You will find that most British people are not skilled in foreign languages and will normally wish to speak to you in English. Although you might find this a little inconvenient when you first arrive, it is in reality a considerable benefit to you. You will find that your progress is much quicker if you speak English the whole time.

Try to get at least a modest knowledge of English before you arrive here. This will make it easier for you to settle down and prevent you from being obliged to speak with fellow employees in your own language - if you once start doing that, it is difficult to stop the practice later on.

You will find that it is useful to take English lessons while you are here. A professional teacher will correct and guide you so that, by the time you leave, you will be able to take pride in your accurate pronunciation and grammar.

Finding a placement

If you are a citizen of one of the countries of the European Community (EC) your first step should be to apply through HOTREC, which is an organization grouping the main National Hotel and Restaurant Associations. Application forms are available either from your National Hotel and Restaurant Association or from :

HOTREC

Bd Anspach 111, bte 4
1000 Bruxelles, Belgium
Tel. 32 2 513 63 23 - Fax 32 2 513 89 54

On the application form you choose three EC countries in order of preference and you can request either a hotel or a restaurant placement. You must normally be aged 18-25 years (in exceptional circumstances, older candidates can be considered) and have completed a basic training either at a college or on-the-job in a hotel or restaurant. The placement can last from three to twelve months and will normally be in the kitchen or in food service. Wages are at a special trainee rate and the employer arranges accommodation for you.

At the end of a successful placement you will receive the ''European Stagiaire Certificate'' and can claim reimbursement of your approved travelling expenses.

If you are not a citizen of an EC country, the above scheme is regrettably not open to you.

An alternative way of finding a placement is to write direct to an employer. Your college may be able to assist you with names and addresses. Other sources of information include hotel and restaurant guides, such as the following :

(1) ''UK Hotel Groups Directory'' by R Collison and K Johnson (published by Cassell Educational Ltd)

(2) ''Hotels and Restaurants of Britain'' (published annually by the British Hospitality Association, 40 Duke Street, London W1M 6HR)

The following is a small selection of major employers :

Forte Hotels :
        166 High Holborn, LONDON WC1V 6TT

Mount Charlotte Thistle Hotels :
        2 The Calls, LEEDS LS2 7JU

Queens Moat Houses :
        9-17 Eastern Road, ROMFORD, Essex RM1 3NG

Hilton International Hotels :
   2/3 Rhodes Way, WATFORD, Herts WD2 4WY

Holiday Inns International :
   62 London Road, STAINES, Middlesex TW18 4JE

Concord Hotels :
   7 Green Road, Terriers, HIGH WYCOMBE, Bucks HP13 5BD

Gardner Merchant Ltd (catering contractors) :
   Kenley House, Kenley Road, KENLEY, Surrey CR2 5ED

Forte Catering :
   Great West House, Great West Road, BRENT-FORD, Middlesex, TW8 9DF

Department of Health-Hotel & Dietetic Services (hospital catering) :
   Hannibal House, Elephant & Castle, LONDON SE1 6TE

This selection of names and addresses is only an illustration of the range of organizations able to offer training. Equally good opportunities are available from a large number of organizations which are not included in the above lists.

When writing to a potential employer, it is advisable to include :

- a photograph : passport size is sufficient, but ensuring that you present a smart, conventional appearance ;
- a statement of the kind of training which you seek and the dates when you are available ;
- details of your age, nationality, marital status, general education, technical training, certificates gained and previous and present employment (if any) ;
- copies (not originals) of any references you may have ;
- an indication of your ability to speak, read and write language.

If the employer is able to offer you a training place, he should inform you of the wages, hours of work and availability of accommodation ; he will also specify any other requirements (eg, a medical certificate). If you are applying through HOTREC, this information forms part of the standard documentation.
For urgent communication, it is worth considering the use of Fax.

Preparations for departure

Work permits and regulations

The following applies to those who are NOT citizens of the EC or the Commonwealth :

(a) A Work Permit must be obtained before entering the UK - apply via your prospective employer.

(b) At the port or airport of entry, you will be asked questions by an Immigration Officer, who will stamp your passport.

(c) You should register within 7 days with the local police, if it is stated in your passport that you should do so. This will entail producing your passport to the police, completing a form, providing 2 passport-size photographs, and paying a registration certificate fee (at present £ 36).

(d) You must tell the police if you change your address, obtain an extension to your permit, or change your marital status.

Citizens of the Commonwealth must comply with the first two paragraphs but are not required to register with the police.
Citizens of the European Community are exempt from most of the above requirements ; they do not need Work Permits, but should inform the Home Office if their stay exceeds 6 months (this requirement may change in 1992). These privileges will not apply fully to citizens of Spain and Portugal until 1992.

As Government regulations can vary from time to time and according to individual circumstances, the foregoing should be regarded as only indicative and trainees should verify the situation when making arrangements for their placement.

Documents and other arrangements

You will need some or all of the following documents :
- passport or identity card (and possibly parental authorization if you are a minor) ;
- National Insurance documents ;
- taxation documents (if any) ;

- placement contract (HOTREC or individual) and correspondence with the employer ;
- personal papers such as health documents (blood group, any special health requirements, etc) and driving licence (if any).

You may also wish to consider taking out :
- public liability insurance (to cover you against claims from other people if you should be the cause of injury to other people or damage to their property) ;
- insurance against loss of your money or personal property ;
- private health insurance.

For all types of insurance, you should seek professional advice to ensure that the of the insurance are appropriate to your individual needs.

The National Health Service in Britain provides free treatment to all eligible persons, covering treatment by a doctor, treatment in hospital and transportation by ambulance. There is a charge for prescriptions and for dental treatment (and for certain other specialized services, such as the provision of glasses), although persons on low incomes may be exempted.

You can expect to receive immediate hospital treatment for a life-threatening illness or in the event of an accident. However, if you require hospital treatment for a less urgent condition, you may have to join a waiting list. It is to avoid the waiting list that some people take out private health insurance, covering the charges for a private hospital bed, surgery and other treatment. There are also other advantages, such as choice of hospital and surgeon.

Private health insurance is not essential but, if you do decide to have it, make sure that will it cover your costs fully - the major hospitals in London and the larger cities charge considerably more than the smaller hospitals elsewhere.

In the event of an accident occurring at work whilst you are performing your normal duties, it is likely that your employer would be liable to pay any costs and (if appropriate) compensation.

Luggage and travel

Kitchen dress is normally similar throughout most of Europe, ie, white jacket ; blue check or white trou-

sers ; neckerchief ; white chef's hat. An apron and sometimes the chef's hat may be provided by the employer. You should, however, enquire before coming about the exact dress requirements for your job.

The climate in Britain is fairly equable, although the weather can occasionally be very hot or very cold. Rain can be expected at any time of year.

You should be aware of the possibility that you may be liable to pay duty on goods which you bring into Britain. Travel agents, or British consulates and embassies, should be able to advise you on duty-free concessions. As you will be working in Britain, you may be able to bring in, without paying duty, items (other than tobacco goods, alcohol and perfume) which you will need for your personal use whilst you are here. It is expected that restrictions on EC citizens will be discontinued after 1992.

If you notify your future employer of the exact time and place of your arrival, you may find that there is someone to meet you. Unless your place of work is near a port or airport, you will probably be expected to go by train to the nearest railway station before being met.

On arrival at your place of work, you should (unless you receive instructions to the contrary) present yourself to the Staff Manager or to the Head Chef.

Accommodation will usually have been arranged for you. If your place of work is a hotel, you are likely to be given a bedroom either within the hotel itself or in a nearby building used for staff accommodation. If it is a restaurant, you are likely to be accommodated externally. In London, your accommodation might be a considerable distance from your place of work. It is usual for meals to be provided free whilst on duty and, if you are living in, all your meals will probably be provided free.

After you have settled in, you should be given, in writing, your conditions of employment (unless you have received this information during previous correspondence). Not every employer, however, complies with this requirement.

The kitchen

Hygiene

Hygiene is essential to the welfare of customers and is so crucial in the eyes of the British public that any outbreak of food poisoning or any successful prosecution for unsanitary conditions can result in a restaurant being driven out of business. Environmental health inspectors visit every kitchen on a regular basis and they can prosecute employers and (if appropriate) individual staff. Hygiene laws in Britain are amongst the strictest in Europe and every trainee must be prepared to comply with them fully. Breaches of hygiene rules can lead to dismissal.

The range of foods and equipment

A wide range of foods is available throughout the year and, with modern methods of preservation and transport, the problem of seasonal availability is now relatively unimportant.

In Britain, there is less emphasis on regional foods than in some other parts of Europe. Most of the foods which bear the name of a particular locality (eg, Aylesbury duck, Manx kipper) are freely available everywhere.

Many of the old-fashioned regional recipes are not particularly popular and are used only on special occasions ; others, in contrast, such as Yorkshire pudding, have become virtually national dishes and are used (often in a modernized form) throughout the country.

There is widespread use of pre-prepared foods ("convenience foods"). These may be complete dishes which have been frozen or chilled, or single ingredients which are frozen, chilled, canned, dehydrated or (occasionally) irradiated. The use of these foods does not necessarily lower the quality of a dish : they can be used artistically and skillfully and can result in high quality products.

Kitchens in Britain are gradually beginning to use a wider variety of cooking equipment. Convection ovens have been in common use for many years, but a wide range of other modern equipment is now beginning to appear.

Kitchen organization

Kitchen organization in Britain varies greatly from one establishment to another.

Until after the Second World War, the classical Continental style of organization was almost universal in good quality hotels and restaurants.

The hierarchy took the following form and French job titles were generally used :

(I) Chef de Cuisine (Head Chef) - responsible for all aspects of the work of the kitchen , including staffing, training, quality control, methods of cooking, work planning, menu creation and financial control.

(II) Sous-Chef (Deputy Head Chef) - except in a very large kitchen, this post would usually be combined with that of a Chef de Partie, such as the Chef Saucier.

(III) A number of Chefs de Partie (Section Chefs) each with their field of responsibility :

- Saucier (Sauce Chef) - sauces and the braising, pot-roasting, sautéing and poaching of poultry, game, meat and (often) fish ;

- Rôtisseur (Roast Chef) - roasting, grilling and frying ;

- Garde-manger (Larder Chef) - control of the cold room, cutting up of raw meats and preparation of cold dishes, including hors d'œuvres ;

- Entremétier - soups, egg dishes, vegetables and hot entrées such as quiches and soufflés ;

- Pâtissier (Pastry Chef) - pastry, ice cream dishes, petits fours and other sweet or dessert dishes ;

- Tournant (Relief Chef) - replacement of other Chefs de Partie in their absence ;

- Communard (Staff Cook) - preparation of staff meals.

(IV) Commis Chefs, apprentices and trainees.

(V) Supporting staff, including kitchen porters - responsible for washing pans, carrying loads and keeping the kitchen clean ; they might also be responsible for the basic cleaning and rough preparation of vegetables.

This hierarchy still exists in a relatively small number of traditional, classical restaurants. Generally, however, even in high quality restaurants, it has been greatly simplified. Vegetables are usually delivered washed and peeled ready for cooking ; meat and fish are supplied cut into portions of specified size ; ice cream (and sometimes pastries) are bought in ; convenience products may assist in the preparation by the Chef of sauces and other components of the meal ; and some complete dishes are bought chilled or frozen and need only to be heated.

With this simplification of work, restaurants need fewer skilled cooks and the work of each member of the team is more diverse.

At the same time, the role of the Head Chef has changed. Many hotels have a Food and Beverage Manager, who is responsible for all aspects of the production and service of food and drinks and who takes over some of the strategic planning role of the Head Chef. Personnel Directors, Training Managers and Purchasing Officers also impinge on the Head Chef's traditional realm. Within hotel and restaurant chains, the functions of layout planning and choice of kitchen equipment are often in the hands of specialists. In popular catering, Head Office directives usually regulate many of the kitchen working pratices and Chefs have to cook according to standard recipes.

Playing your part

Make sure you benefit...

In order to get full benefit from your training, you should seek experience in as many parts of the kitchen as possible. Hopefully your contract will have included a training plan, which will ensure that you are regularly moved round the various sections. If this does not happen, do not hesitate to ask the Head Chef, explaining that you wish to learn as much as possible. If you are aiming ultimately at a management career, you could request also short periods with the Food and Beverage Manager (if there is one), the Stores or Purchasing Office, and the section in the Accounts Office where the kitchen finances are controlled.

It is useful to keep a log book in which you can make notes of your observations and queries. You will find

that you get the greatest benefit from your placement if you think analytically about the various situations you observe. For example :

- How is the work of each section organized ? Is it efficient ?

- Is there the right number of staff, or too many or too few ? and do they have the right skills for the jobs they do ?

- Are the staff hard-working and well-motivated ? If not, what is going wrong (is it their working conditions, the way they are treated, or some other cause ?)

- Is the staffing structure right for this situation ?

- Is there enough kitchen equipment of the right kind ?

- How can "convenience foods" be best used ? Should they be despised or is there a role for them ?

- Is the food presented on the dish or plate in an attractive way ?

- How is a high standard of hygiene assured ?

- Is there harmony between the kitchen staff and the waiters ?

- Is the restaurant as busy, or busier, than other comparable restaurants in the locality ? If not, what might be the reason (type of menu, quality of food, quality of service, price, location of the restaurant, etc) ?

Although some of these questions are difficult to answer, you will find that the mere fact of thinking about them will make you much more aware of what is happening around you. As you move in the future from one employment to another, you will be able to compare the way they operate and their relative success. This will give you an excellent basis for advancement in your career - the higher you go up the career ladder, the more this kind of awareness becomes a key to your success. But, at this stage in your career, be diplomatic : do not ask awkward questions which might make your companions or superiors feel that you are being critical or trying to be too "clever". It is often better to observe, think and analyse silently to yourself.

... And create the right impression

It is important to create the right impression on your superiors. The hotel and restaurant industry is like a worldwide fraternity and your superiors will almost certainly be able and willing, if they think highly of you, to recommend you to their colleagues when you wish to take the next step up the promotion ladder.

You should, therefore, pay attention to the following :

- your appearance should be smart and conventional (traditional hairstyle and clothing, no earrings or other ornaments for men) ;
- you should be punctual in arriving but always willing to stay on duty late if the business requires it ;
- whilst there is no reason for being underpaid, you should remember that it is more important to get the right training than to seek the highest possible salary ;
- always make people (whether superiors or colleagues) feel that you respect them : ask their advice and seek their knowledge ;
- work hard and learn each job as quickly and effectively as possible ;
- show enthusiasm and initiative.

After your placement is finished, keep in touch with the Managers and Head Chefs under whom you have trained - they may be willing to help you in years to come.

You can help yourself also by getting part-time education during your placement. Information on educational opportunities is given in the next section.

Educational opportunities

Enrolling on a course

Practically every sizeable town in Britain has a Technical College which offers catering courses. For people working in the kitchen, these courses usually lead to a certificate awarded by the City and Guilds of London Institute (''City and Guilds''). The courses are at various levels, starting from the most basic and going up to the Master Certificate. They can be taken by part-time attendance at College (eg, one day or two half-days or evenings per week) and are very flexible in their attendance and assessment arrangements. The student takes a series of units showing his/her competence and these can be accumulated towards the award of a National Vocational Qualification (NVQ).

Discuss with your employer the possibility of attending a course - many employers would welcome such an initiative on your part and might be willing to pay the College fees.

The national picture

You will find that many - but by no means all - of your colleagues will have some kind of qualification, but many of the more senior staff did not have the same opportunities and have based their success only on practical experience. However, nowadays almost every new entrant who aims at a craft or management career studies for a qualification, and you may well find yourself working alongside a student from one of the following courses :

City & Guilds Certificates in Restaurant Service, Housekeeping or Hotel Reception

Business & Technician Education Concil (BTEC) National Diploma or Higher National Diploma

Hotel, Catering and Institutional Management Association (HCIMA) Professional Certificate or Diploma
BSc or BA degree from a University or Polytechnic

Further Professional Development

How can you take your professional development to the furthest point of which you are capable ? You will already be working hard in the kitchen, thinking carefully about what you are observing, asking questions, perhaps attending a part-time College course. One thing more will be of benefit to you - to read at least one trade journal and some of the more important and relevant books.

The main trade journal is :

"Caterer and Hotelkeeper" (weekly)
Reed Business Publishing, The Quadrant, SUTTON SM2 5AS

There are a large number of professional books which you could find helpful. The following IS a small selection originating in the English language :

V Ceserani, D E Lundberg and L H Kotschevar :
Understanding Cooking (Edward Arnold)

V Ceserani, R Kinton and D Foskett :
Contemporary Cookery (Edward Arnold)

H Cracknell and G Nobis :
Practical Professional Gastronomy (Macmillan)

Useful addresses :

HCIMA,
191 Trinity Road, LONDON, SW17 7HN

Chefs & Cooks Circle,
PO Box 239, LONDON, N14 7NT

Craft Guild of Chefs,
1 Victoria Parade, 331 Sandycombe Road,
RICHMOND, Surrey TW9 3NB

Hotel & Catering Benevolent Association,
52 Ridgeway, Wimbledon,
LONDON, SW19 4QR (Telephone 081-946-7561)

The main hotel and catering exhibition is "HOTELYMPIA" which takes place every 2 years (in the even-numbered year) at the Olympia Exhibition Centre in London.

Enjoying everyday life in Britain

You will want to integrate as quickly as possible into British life and enjoy your free time to the maximum. Here are some useful items of information to help you to do this.

Eating and drinking

Traditionally, breakfast is a major meal and includes fruit juice or cereal, bacon and egg, toast, butter and marmalade, together with tea or coffee. Many families, however, now eat a very light breakfast consisting of only one of these foods.

Sunday lunch is usually the main family meal of the week and includes a roast joint of beef, lamb or pork.

Wine is not usually drunk with meals at home, but sales are increasing rapidly and it is now common to drink wine with main meals in restaurants. You should, incidentally, take the opportunity to try English wine, which is produced in the Southern half of England. It is of good quality, almost always white, and resembles in character the wines of the Rhine ; prices are within the medium range. English wine should not be confused with "British Wine" - a cheap drink made from imported unfermented grape juice. The most widely consumed spirit is Scotch whisky, followed by gin and rum ; sales of rum have recently begun to increase rapidly. Wine-based "aperitifs" are not popular and the sale of most eaux-de-vie and sweetened liqueurs is very small.

Shopping and telephoning

Most shops are now open every day of the week except Sunday. The usual closing time is 5.00 pm or 6.00 pm, but some major stores remain open until later on at least one day per week. Chemists (pharmacies) keep normal shop hours, but in every town one chemist remains open until late in the evening and on Sunday morning - a rota for this late duty is usually displayed in the doorway of every chemists shop.

Banks usually close at 3.30 pm, and do not open on Saturdays (there are some exceptions to this general pratice). Many building societies now offer cheque book facilities to their customers and are open for longer hours than the banks. Both operate cash dispensing machines.

You should register as soon as possible with a doctor and a dentist for treatment within the provisions of the National Health Service.

For telephoning, you will find it useful to buy a "Phonecard" - these are on sale from many kiosks and shops. About half the public telephone boxes take only Phonecards and will not accept money.

Sightseeing

Britain has a great deal to offer by way of beautiful scenery, fine stately homes, castles, cathedrals, museums, art galleries and other places of interest. You can travel economically by using long-distance coaches (which are much cheaper than standard train fares). If you are eligible, you can buy a Student Rail Card which will give you a discount of one-third on most train fares.

Gifts

If you are looking for a typical British product to take home as a gift, here are some ideas : Scotch whisky (there are a great variety of blends, ages - and prices !) ; English wine ; Stilton cheese ; farm-made blue Wensleydale cheese (not easy to find) ; Scotch smoked salmon ; speciality teas ; Sheffield-made scissors ; bone china ; cut glass (30 % lead crystal) ; woollen sweaters, cardigans, etc (Marks and Spencer are well known suppliers).

Departing

When getting ready to leave, ensure that you remember to return any books, knives, etc, that you may have been lent. Ask for a reference, which you can keep for future use. If you do not have a new post to go to, you may find that the Head Chef or the Manager has connections which can help your search for employment.

Finally, thank all those who have helped you and advised you, not least the Head Chef. Even if you have seen very little of the General Manager during your placement, it will be appreciated if you ask for an appointment to see him to express your gratitude. And, after you have left, make sure that you keep in touch.

No doubt you will retain happy memories of your colleagues - and they will retain happy memories of you !

— 2 —
in
FRANCE
[F]

by

Sylvaine Bouquerel
Maîtrise en Hôtellerie-Restauration
Training Adviser

and

Serge Perrot
Agrégé de l'Université
Formerly Regional Inspector of Education

Translation by
Professor Derek C. Gladwell
OBE, MA, FHCIMA, FRSA

Before you leave

So you want to train in France !
First, you should know that French law, unlike that of other countries, draws a clear distinction between a traineeship and employment.

• *A traineeship (« stage »)* lasts for two to six months and is an integral part of a college course, taking place after the course starts but before the final examinations. Trainees receive a modest allowance, rather than a wage, and their working conditions and national insurance arrangements are set out in a training agreement signed by the college and the organization offering the training. Supervised work experience, which forms part of a sandwich course, falls within this definition.

• All other work is defined as **employment (« emploi »).** It is subject to normal employment legislation covering wages, insurance contributions and income tax and the conditions are set out in a contract of employment between the employer and the employee.

Finding a placement

Whether you are seeking a traineeship or employment, you should start your planning well in advance, as the arrangements can take up to six months to complete.

• If you are taking a sandwich course, you should apply through your college. Otherwise, the normal first step for a UK citizen is to apply through :
The British Hospitality Association (BHA, formerly BHRCA)

40 Duke Street, LONDON WIM 6HR
Telephone : 071-499-6641

The BHA runs a scheme on behalf of HOTREC, which is an international organization consisting of the main national Hotel and Restaurant Associations within the European Community (EC). On the application form, you choose three EC countries in order of preference and you can request either a hotel or a restaurant placement. You must normally be aged 18-25 years (in exceptional circumstances, older candidates can be considered) and have completed a basic training either at a college or on-the-job in a hotel or restaurant. The placement can last from three to twelve months and will normally be in the kitchen or in food service. Wages are at an agreed rate and the employer arranges accommodation for you.

At the end of a successful placement, you will receive the « European Stagiaire Certificate » and can claim reimbursement of your approved travelling expenses from the organizers of the scheme.

• If you are a citizen of an EC country other than the UK, you should apply either to your National Hotel and Restaurant Association or direct to :

HOTREC

Bd Anspach 111, bte 4
1000 Bruxelles, Belgique
Tel. 32 2 513 63 23 - Fax 32 2 513 89 54

If you are not a citizen of an EC country, the above scheme is regrettably not open to you.

An alternative way of finding a placement is to write directly to an employer. Your college may be able to assist you with names and addresses.

Naturally, you will already have studied French and you should take every opportunity to develop your skill in speaking it. You will find that the following are useful :

- courses at the Alliance Française or the Centre Culturel Français ;
- French language lessons on tape (your present college may be able to advise you) ;
- French films and television/radio broadcasts.

Making the application

As soon as you have been put in touch with an employer, you should make a written application. This should include :

- your curriculum vitae (typewritten) with a photograph (pay attention to your dress and hair style ; male candidates should wear a tie) ;
- a short letter of application (in you own handwriting) stating your aims and the dates when you would be available ;

- copies of any references you may have from previous jobs or training placements.

Request information from the employer on :

- the nature of the post offered to you, its duration and a proposed starting date ;
- the conditions of employment, ie, whether accommodation, meals and laundry will be provided ; what your wages will be and what your take-home pay will be after deductions ; whether, if accommodation is not provided, the employer will find lodgings for you and what they are likely to cost ;
- your situation with regard to social security, accident insurance and health insurance ;
- administrative details, such as telephone, telex and fax numbers.

If your placement is an official traineeship (ie, a « stage »), pass this information to your college authorities, who will arrange with your prospective employer for the signing of the training agreement and will pass a copy to you. If it is classed as employment (ie, « emploi ») and not a traineeship, you yourself may be responsible for the arrangements. Remember that fax can be useful in speeding up negotiations.

Formal arrangements

• Before your departure, give careful thought to all the papers, formalities and precautions which may be necessary.

1 Papers and documents :
- identity card or passport (and parental authorization if you are a minor) ;
- national health insurance documents ;
- the training agreement/employment contract/letter from your prospective employer or the HOTREC document ;
- personal documents, such as your medical papers, a note of your blood group, driving licence (if any), etc;
- public liability insurance certificate (to cover you against claims made by other people, if you should be the cause of injury to them or damage to their property).

If your placement lasts longer than three months, you

will need a long stay visa (« visa de long séjour »), obtainable from the French embassy or consulate. The following are exempt from this requirement :

- citizens of countries in the European Community (except Portugal and Spain until 1992);
- citizens of Algeria and Switzerland.

2 Clothing : you will need :
- working clothes ;
- a raincoat and warm clothing for the cooler weather.

3 Personal preparation :
- study the rest of this book and read as much as possible about the area of France to which you are going. You will need confidence, curiosity, and a determination to succeed. Remember that the training will only be as good as you make it.

• At the French frontier, there will be a minimum of formalities. Nevertheless, you should take care to comply with the regulations, such as the maximum permitted quantities of cigarettes and alcohol. Small personal gifts are allowed.

• When you arrive, there will certainly be someone waiting to meet you, with a sign bearing your name, provided that you have given full details of the date, time and place of your arrival (railway station, coach station, airport).

When you reach your place of employment, report to the Manager or to the Head Chef. You will be shown the accommodation reserved for you, which may be in the establishment itself or lodgings outside. You will also be given a copy of the House Rules, if such a document is available. You should as soon as possible clarify your situation regarding social security.

Personal accident and health insurance

• Your training agreement (between your college and your employer) or your contract of employment (between your employer and you or your parents) will specify the terms and conditions of your traineeship, including its duration, hours of work, salary or allowance, and insurance cover.

• If your employer has not enrolled you in the National Insurance scheme, you can enrol yourself in order to be covered (ask for advice on the steps you should take).

Accidents at work

• It is the responsibility of the employer to have insurance cover for accidents at work.

• You may have a liability under civil law if you cause an accident and it is therefore essential for you to take out insurance against this possibility before leaving home.

Termination of your traineeship

If you find that it is impossible to continue with your training placement (eg because of abnormal working conditions, intolerable surroundings, or health problems), you should inform the college or other body which arranged the placement and politely request that the placement be terminated. If, on the other hand, you have committed a serious act of misconduct (eg, breach of disciplinary rules or breach of security), the employer can terminate the placement, after informing your college.

On the job

Training can vary considerably according to the size of the establishment. Some employers offer an induction period lasting several days and a highly organized training programme.

Your adventure is now beginning. Whether or not it will become a memorable experience depends entirely on you. The French believe, rightly or wrongly, that they are amongst the world's finest cooks. For centuries, cookery and gastronomy have been part of their culture, closely linked with their religion, their history, their traditions, their sense of well-being and their way of life. Their culinary skills, of which they are so proud and which are the subject of daily conversation, are to them an ART - an exacting, rigorous ART, which demands devoted and loving attention. It is an art which relies on respect for basic principles, on a great variety of cookery traditions, on a mastery of stocks and sauces, and on a highly developed sense of taste and gastronomic culture.

The phenomenon of convenience food, which has influenced France as it has other countries, has served only to reinforce the value of classical cooking as a point of reference, with its emphasis on the importance of basic recipes, the role of the kitchen brigade and the prestige of the Chef - which is symbolized by his « toque » (distinctive hat).

This is the world that you will enter, most probably as a commis cook. If you want to make the most of your opportunities, you would be well advised to :

- show interest, curiosity and enthusiasm for everything you do ;
- accept with good grace the authority of the Chef (remember the saying « the Chef is always right ») ; be flexible, adaptable, patient and humble ; and always conduct yourself correctly ;
- never get involved in other people's problems or quarrels ;
- give unstintingly of your time and your efforts.

The kitchen brigade

All well-run kitchens have a similar organizational hierarchy based on sections («parties »), each corresponding to a specialized field of production.

You should know how a brigade is organized. In a traditional establishment, a full brigade consists of :

Management - linking the kitchen with the restaurant

The Chef
Deputy Chef («Sous Chef»)

Principal sections	**Secondary sections**
Sauce Chef («Saucier»)	Grill Chef («Grillardin»)
Roast Chef («Rôtisseur»)	Fish Chef
Larder Chef («Garde Manger»)	(«Poissonnier»)
«Chef Entremétier»	
Pastry Chef («Patissier»)	

Relief Chef («Tournant»)
Staff Chef («Communard»)
Junior Cooks («Commis»), apprentices and trainees

The Chef is in full charge of organization and production.

• He appoints the staff and ensures that they are trained, motivated and developed ; he allocates and supervises the work of the kitchen.

- He is responsible for the food stocks, the budget and the financial results.
- He oversees the planning of the menus, the maintenance of quality standards, and the encouragement of creativity and innovation.

The Sauce Chef is the Section Chef responsible for the most delicate work ; he needs a highly developed sense of taste. He makes the stocks and sauces, and is responsible for the braising, pot-roasting, sautéing and poaching of poultry and meat (and also of fish if there is no separate Fish Chef).

The Roast Chef deals with all foods (meat, poultry, game and vegetables) which are oven-roasted, spit-roasted, grilled or fried ; he is usually supported by a specialist Grill Chef for quick-grill items (steaks, chops).

The Larder Chef receives, controls and holds the foods supplied from the stores ; he is responsible for the cold room and the distribution of its contents ; he cuts and portions meat ; and he prepares cold dishes. He may be assisted by a Butcher and an Hors-d'œuvre Chef.

The Chef Entremétier (sometimes, but inadequately, translated into English as Vegetable Chef) is responsible for soups, egg dishes, vegetables (except those which are grilled or fried), hot entrees (gnocchis, quiches, soufflés) and, in the absence of the Pastry Chef, sweet dishes (cream caramel, pancakes, sweet soufflés). He is sometimes assisted by a Soup Chef.

The Pastry Chef in a restaurant has a wider role than his counterpart in a shop. In addition to pastry dishes, ice cream dishes, sorbets and «petits fours», he normally prepares the sweet dishes and any doughs or batters for the kitchen. He may be assisted by an ice cream specialist.

In addition to these principal and secondary section chefs, there is the **Relief Chef** (who replaces the section chefs during their meal breaks) and the **Staff Chef** who prepares the staff meals.

The brigade in the restaurant where you train may be much smaller than this, but all the above roles will be carried out and it will be in your interest to learn about as many of them as possible.

If you want to be moved to another part of the kitchen, make your request diplomatically :

« Chef (that is how he should be addressed), I have been in the larder since I arrived - could I move to another section so that I can learn as much as possible ? »

You will learn not only by *doing* the job, but also by observing, thinking, asking questions and making notes. Keep a notebook, so that you can record each evening those things which, during the day, seemed important to you or which you did not understand. Later you can seek an explanation.

Refer to books and articles (see page 41), which will help you to develop your knowledge.
You will soon begin to notice the points of comparison with your own country :

• In the tempo of work, traditions, and working practices. Officially, you will work 43 hours a week, with a maximum of 11 hours in any one day, and you will have at least one-and-a-half days off per week. This may seem hard at first, especially during periods of peak pressure - but do not crack under the strain. Most of the famous restaurants still insist on compliance with strict disciplinary rules :

- punctuality (« time is time ») ;

- discipline at the work place : no chatting and no smoking in the kitchen ;

- respect and consideration for the Chef ;

- personal appearance (cleanliness and short hair) and correct dress (chefs hat or « toque » ; knotted neckerchief ; white jacket, trousers and apron ; kitchen rubber held at your side).

• In the organization and methods of work : for example, the importance of careful workplace preparation ; the use of mobile and fixed work stations ; and an obsession with neatness.

• In the equipment and technical installations. France is often in the vanguard in this respect. Every kitchen has refrigeration (+ 4°C) and freezing (-18° to -24°C) capacity and various types of oven (eg. fan-convection ovens). Even classical restaurants often have induction cookers and many use the « sous-vide » system (in which food is placed in a sealed vacuum bag, then cooked and chilled, and finally reheated when needed for service). Some have even reached the stage of « combination cookery » in which they use a mixture of fresh, preserved (bottled), frozen and sous-vide (4 th and 5 th range) components. Ask for this to be explained to you.

• In food legislation, which is very strict in France. Ask for an explanation of the regulations covering :
- the storage of foodstuffs (Decree of 26 September 1980) ;
- the correct flow path of foods within the kitchen : uncleaned foods must not enter the area used for prepared foods (Decree of 26 September 1980) ;
- the holding of cooked foods before service (Decree of 26 June 1984)

• In the preparation of the dishes themselves. You probably came with a preconception of what French cooking is like :
- compare your previous ideas with what you are practising now and use your reference books to relate the latter to basic principles ;
- find out about alternative methods and about regional cooking ;
- seek an opportunity to learn about creative cookery and the art of tasting ;
- take an interest in the presentation of dishes and the different kinds of service : French service (rare in commercial catering), English service, Russian service, plate service, etc. Respect and learn from what you see in the skills of presentation, the style of « nouvelle cuisine », and everything relating to the art of the table.

Get the best out of your stay

By means of questions, reading and visits, you should make yourself as familiar as possible with everything relating to your profession - and also get to know the French people and their way of life. This will benefit your personal, as well as your professional, development.

The following information will be useful to you when you start.

The eating habits of the French

Traditionally, the French regard the midday and the evening meals as the most important. They spend 45 minutes to an hour on each and they like to be seated while eating. Ideally, they prefer a full meal, shared with the family, friends or colleagues in a convivial atmosphere.

Breakfast (between 6.30 am and 8.30 am, according to working hours) is usually light : coffee (with milk), bread, butter and jam. On Sundays, whether at home or in a cafe, there may also be croissants. The croissant, like the baker's shop, is a traditional feature of French gastronomy. Apart from a wide range of French breads (of which the « baguette » is the most famous), a plethora of Viennese breads can be found - bread with chocolate, currant bread, milk bread, brioches, etc.

Lunch (between 12.30 and 2.00 pm) is a full meal of four courses : a starter (raw vegetables, plate of cold meats, etc), a main dish (fish or meat with vegetables), cheese, and sweet or fruit. Although wine is the usual drink. there is a tendency, especially with the younger generation, for it to be replaced by water at the midday meal.

Dinner (usually 7.00 pm to 9.00 pm, but in some restaurants up to 11.00 pm or midnight) is often less heavy than lunch but still includes three or four dishes : soup or hors-d'œuvre, a main course (such as a

dish « au gratin » or a soufflé), a salad and/or a dessert.

You will discover the great variety of French cheeses and wines, and the abundance of vegetables and fruits available. You will learn of the importance of offal (liver, kidney, tripe, sweetbreads, tongue, etc) in French cooking. You probably already know that the French love snails and frogs legs and that they eat a lot of seafood and shellfish. However, eating habits are gradually changing, especially in the big cities, due to the increase in sedentary work, the shortening of meal breaks, longer journeys between home and work, and changing attitudes (ecological concerns, diet consciousness, and care for the quality of life). At midday many office staff now have only a sandwich or a snack, or they eat in the firm's canteen.

The famous, traditional high standards of French cooking are carried on, in their different ways, in three kinds of situation :

• Celebration meals (with family, friends, colleagues, etc) arranged at home or at a restaurant on the occasion of a wedding, anniversary, confirmation, etc ; they are formal in character, last for several hours and include a great array of dishes.

The pre-meal drink (of kir, aniseed aperitif, port, whisky or champagne) is served with tit-bits, such as olives, dried fruits, savoury biscuits, etc.

In former times, the menu would consist of five or six courses (starter, fish, roast and/or a dish with sauce, cheese, dessert), accompanied by three different wines. The tendency nowadays, in the towns, is towards lighter meals and it is becoming common to have only four courses, with one or two wines. Some speciality dishes are linked with particular festivals :

Epiphany (in January) : Twelfth Night cake
Candlemas (in February) : pancakes
Easter : paschal lamb and kidney beans ; Easter eggs
Christmas and New Year's Eve : oysters, white sausage, foie gras, turkey with chestnuts, Yule log.

• The highest level of cookery, which is found in the starred restaurants and used for business entertaining or the more intimate type of celebration, has increased in prestige with the fashion for « nouvelle cuisine », which was introduced in the 1970's by Bocuse, Troisgros, Guérard, etc. Even though the fashion has waned, the trend has continued - towards lightness, variety, originality, quality of presentation, and exotic inspiration. This is the kind of cooking which the leading exponents of French culinary art are exporting to America, Japan and, indeed, the whole world.

• Regional cookery. In contrast to sophisticated « haute cuisine », each region of France has retained, and often developed and emphasised, its own homely style of cooking, based on locally-grown foods.

French cooking has kept local differentiations arising from, for example, the cooking medium (butter, oil or lard) and the choice of seasonings (garlic, onion or shallot) despite the fact that some local specialities have become national dishes (eg, pot-au-feu, petit salé, blanquette and calf's head) and many products (cheeses, breads, pork-butchery dishes, wines, etc) are universally available.

The West of France (Brittany, Normandy, Pays de Loire, Vendée and Charente) boasts varied sea products (fish, crustaceans, shellfish), salt-meadow lamb («agneau pré-salé ») and cider. Brittany uses demisel butter, whilst Normandy prefers cream. Specialities include lobster armoricaine, Breton pancakes and galettes, Normandy tripe and pork sausage, and Rouen duck.

The South-West (Aquitaine, Midi-Pyrénées and Périgord) is a particularly rich area with truffles, game, mushrooms, foie gras ; the wines of Bordeaux, the brandies of Cognac and Armagnac ; and the prunes of Agen. Specialities include : cassoulet ; traditionally-preserved fruit, vegetables and meat ; baron of lamb ; Bayonne ham.

The South-East (Languedoc, Provence and the Côte d'Azur) offers fish soups, bouillabaisse, aïoli and ratatouille.
Savoy, Dauphiné, Lyonnais and Burgundy are often considered to be the gastronomic heartland of France. Lyon is at the centre of a region famed for its pork butchery (Lyon sausage, hot cervelas), its fish (eel stew, quenelles of pike), its Bresse poultry, its Savoy specialities (fondue and gratin dauphinois) and, of course, its cheeses and wines.

The East (Alsace-Lorraine) is celebrated for its sauerkraut, onion tart, quiche Lorraine, and chicken « au

Riesling ». The Ardennes has its leg of venison and its famous wine, Champagne.

The North (Flanders, Artois, Picardy) is known for its very distinctive cheeses (Maroilles, Boulette d'Avesnes) and its special country dishes such as roast pork with apples, tongue of beef, leek flan.

There are two quite distinct regions in the centre of France :

- the Massif Central (Auvergne) with its very homely style of cooking : civet of beef, pork ragoût, salted pork with cabbage or lentils, Auvergne soup, aligot, and black pudding with chestnuts.
- the fashionable Loire Valley, where the gentle climate, the rich soil, and the abundant fish in the rivers and game in the forests has led from early times to the development of refined, high quality dishes : pike au beurre blanc, asparagus with mousseline sauce, game pie. From the 16th century, by building their palaces here and attracting the finest chefs, the kings of France contributed to the birth of the arts of cooking and dining.

The different types of specifically French restaurants

Apart from the luxury restaurants, themed restaurants, cafeterias, pizza parlours, steakhouses, snack bars and pubs, which are similar to those in other countries. There are several types of restaurant that are distinctively French :

• The country house hotel (« château-hôtel » or « relais ») always offers superb cooking and service in a luxurious (and often authentically historical) setting. It provides very good training opportunities.

• The brasserie, which originated in Paris, is now found in every large town : it is a combined cafe and restaurant. Service is traditional but fast and the cooking is simple but distinctive : eg, sauerkraut, pot-au-feu, shellfish, etc. Anything from a single dish to a complete meal is served at any time of day.

• The « bistro » is very much in vogue. With (often) Revival décor (1900-1920) and a relaxed atmosphere, it usually offers a simple, essentially French, style of food ; if the Chef is well-known, prices can be relatively high. Sometimes a « bistro » is the popular annex of a top-flight restaurant, and benefits from the latter's reputation.

• The pancake house (« crêperie »). Originally Breton, the crêperie offers a menu of pancakes and galettes with a variety of garnishes. They may or may not be prepared in front of the customer. They are served at table, usually accompanied by cider.

• The farm restaurant (« ferme-auberge »). Located in a rural setting, farm restaurants offer a limited menu of local foods produced on the farm itself. They are found mainly in Auvergne, Alsace and Brittany.

Famous names in the culinary art of France.

• Great chefs of the past :

Taillevent (whose real name was Guillaume Tirel) was cook to the Kings of France in the 14 th century and wrote the first book on cooking - « Le Viandier ».

La Varenne wrote « Le Cuisinier Français » in 1661.

Antonin Carême was chef to Napoleon, and later to the British Court, to the Emperor of Austria and to the Tsar of Russia. He was the most illustrious chef of the 19th century.

Auguste Escoffier, who worked with César Ritz (of the Savoy and Carlton Hotels in London, the Ritz in Paris, and the Grand Hotel at Monte Carlo), transformed the art of cookery at the beginning of the 20 th century. He was called « the king of chefs and the chef of kings ». The Escoffier Museum is at Villeneuve-Loubet, near Nice.

• The gastronomes (men of letters and distinguished gourmets who have devoted their literary talent to the culinary arts) :

Brillat-Savarin born at Belley (near the Swiss frontier). His principal work « The Physiology of Taste » (1825) is a philosophical treatise on the culinary arts. A seminar, known as the « Entretiens de Belley », is held every year and brings together chefs, gastronomes and scientists to discuss developments in the field of cookery.

Curnonsky, who was elected « Prince of Gastronomes » by 3000 chefs, wrote « La France Gastronomique » and founded the Academy of Gastronomes.

• The great chefs of today are widely known ; amongst the most famous are :

Paul Bocuse - of the Restaurant Bocuse, near Lyon.

Pierre Troisgros - at Roanne

Haeberlin - in Alsace

Robuchon - of « Le Jamin » in Paris.

Michel Guérard - at Eugénie les Bains

Gaston Lenôtre - of « Le Pré Catelan » in Paris.

• The competition for the title « Meilleur Ouvrier de France » (MOF) - ie, Best Artisan of France - in the field of cookery takes place once every four years. From amongst the hundreds of candidates, the best in each region are selected for the final test in Paris. The few who are successful are awarded this prestigious title by the President of the Republic himself, at a formal ceremony in the Great Amphitheatre of the Sorbonne.

Hotel and culinary training in France

It will be of interest to you to know how your colleagues at work have been trained. There are several routes into the culinary profession :

• An apprenticeship, starting at 16 years of age for a period of two years, in a restaurant or hotel, under the supervision of a recognized trainer. The apprentice simultaneously studies for one or two days per week at a specialized school (Centre de Formation d'Apprentis). The training leads to the CAP qualification (Certificat d'Aptitude Professionnelle), which enables the holder to get on to the first rung of the ladder as a « commis de cuisine ». The number following the apprenticeship route has decreased over the last 20 years, but most of the leading chefs of today were trained in this way.

• It is becoming more and more common for the preferred route to be through a full-time college course at a « Lycée d'Enseignement Professionel » (LEP). Students start the two-year course at the age of 15 or 16, after four years of secondary schooling. The core of the curriculum is general restaurant operations, with a specialization in cookery in the second year. The qualification to which it leads is the Brevet d'Etude Professionnelle (BEP), which is at a slightly higher level than the CAP. At the end of the course, the student's first post is that of « commis » but he/she is likely to stay at that level for a shorter period than those who have the CAP.

• Holders of a BEP (and the best amongst the holders of a CAP) can now progress after a further two years to the « baccalauréat professionel » in restaurant operation, which permits a deeper study of culinary techniques. The training is organized on a split basis, half at an LEP and half at the workplace. It makes it possible for the holder to climb the career ladder more quickly.

Cookery can also be studied as part of a training for a hotel career ; there are several levels :

• The Brevet de Technicien de l'Hôtellerie (BTH) can be started at the age of 16 or 17 years, after four or five years of secondary schooling. The course comprises three years at a Lycée Technique Hôtelier and includes a major study of cookery. It leads to supervisory posts in smaller hotels (of up to about 50 rooms).

• The Brevet de Technicien Supérieur (BTS) can be started after the BTH at the age of 19 or 20 years. It lasts for two years and successful students then have one year of management orientation. The course is directed towards management but includes operational kitchen studies. It leads to posts of head of department in large units or to management in hotels of up to about 200 rooms.

• Even courses at the highest academic level can include a study of restaurant management :
- the degree in catering production and management at the Hotel Schools of Toulouse and Strasbourg (Maîtrise de Sciences et Techniques) ;
- the course in « Food and Beverage Management » at the Cornell-Essec International Institute of Hotel Management at Cergy-Pontoise.

Free time and visits

Take advantage of your leisure time to get to know your own locality. France is rich in historical sites and monuments and in its cultural heritage (museums, exhibitions, etc). Ask around and consult the local Tourist Office for information on cultural and touristic visits, including the vineyards.

General Information

• Post offices are open from 8.30 am to 12.00 noon and from 1.30 pm to 6.30 pm during the week, and until 12.00 noon on Saturdays.

• To telephone another country, you dial 19, wait for the correct tone, then dial the code of the country (UK 44, Germany 49, Spain 34, Italy 39) followed by the town code and the number you are calling. It is convenient to buy a « telephone card » ; these are on sale at post offices and tobacconist's shops and can be used in public telephone boxes.

• Banks are closed two days per week (usually Saturdays and Sundays) ; their opening hours are 9.00 am to 5.00 pm, and, in major towns, they do not close for the lunch hour.

• Stores are open from 9.00 to 12.30 pm and from 2.00 pm to 7.00 pm. In Paris and the big conurbations, they do not close in the middle of the day. As a rule, they are closed on Sundays and some are also closed on Mondays. Do not miss seeing the food departments in the big stores and supermarkets - especially the wines and cheeses !
If you are in the vicinity of one of the luxury grocery stores, do not fail to pay it a visit. In Paris, there are Fauchon and Hédiard, both in the Place de la Madeleine they are an Aladdin's cave of exotic products and top-of-the-range foods. But it is the markets that will give you the most typical picture of gastronomic France. There is a market in every small town and you will find many restaurant managers and chefs going in person to choose the locally-produced vegetables, poultry, game or fish. It is a paradise of freshness, colour and interest. Remember to take your camera. In Paris, ask to go with the buyer to the Central Markets (Halles Centrales de Rungis). You will have to get up early but you will never forget the experience - and it will help you to understand better the basis on which the quality of French cooking is built.

Before returning home

You are coming to the end of a period of training which will have been a rich personal and cultural experience for you. It will be a trump card, which will enhance your value to an employer and improve your career prospects. Are you sure that you have extracted the maximum benefit from your stay ? Look through your notes and do not hesitate to ask questions. Is there still any information or documentation for you to collect, which would be useful to you later on ?

Here are some thoughts :

• The trade press. Have you looked through and taken down details of the professional journals ? : You might wish one day (or even now) to keep in touch with what is happening in French hotels and restaurants by taking out a subscription to one or other of these journals. Have a look through them to see which ones interest you - your Chef will advise you.

You should be aware that there are some newspapers, unconnected with the profession, that carry good features on food subjects :

- l'hôtellerie - weekly
  9, rue Ybry, 92200 Neuilly-sur-Seine

- Néo-Restauration - twice a month
  6, rue Marius Aufan, 92300 Levallois-Perret

- Revue Technique des Hôtels et Restaurants
- monthly
  10, rue Beffroy, 92200 Neuilly-sur-Seine

- Revue culinaire - monthly
  45, rue St Roch, 75001 Paris

• Gastronomic guides have an important role, as they classify restaurants. You should know about :

- Guide MICHELIN : a very rigorous classification by stars (3, 2 or 1)

- GAULT and MILLAU : classification using the fork symbol

• A number of specialized exhibitions are held such as EQUIPHOTEL.

• There are a great number of professional books : These books are most easily bought in France, but can if necessary be ordered from a bookshop in your own country.

- « le Livre de l'Apprenti Cuisinier » de R. Pruilhière et R. Lallemand.

- « Le Répertoire de la Cuisine » de Th. Gringoire et Saulnier.

- « La Technologie Culinaire à la Carte » - J.P. Legland/J.M. Wolff

- « Les Nouvelles Bases de la Cuisine » J. Planche/J. Sylvestre
- « La cuisine : Tradition et Techniques Nouvelles » - E Neirinck/J. Planche/J. Sylvestre
- « Le Livre de l'Apprenti Pâtissier » J.P. Deschamps/J.C. Deschaintre
- « Technologie culinaire » M. Maincent

• Useful addresses :
- Employment agencies (if you need to find a post after your period of training) :
- Hôtel Assistance : 11, rue de Clichy, 75009 Paris
- Hôtel Assistance : 6, rue Duhamel, 69002 Lyon
- AIH (International Hôtels Association) : 80, rue de la Roquette, 75544 Paris Cedex 11

Purchases

Trainees sometimes wish to take back with them some of the small professional items which they have found useful, such as a set of patisserie tools or some kitchen knives. If this is the case, ask the Chef for advice.

And if you wish to give some presents, a good bottle of wine, a small tin of foie gras or a book on French cooking will always give pleasure.

When you are ready to leave, remember to :

- go and thank the Manager and everyone who has helped you or been kind to you during your stay ;
- collect a Certificate of Employment (which you should have requested a few days beforehand) ;
- return any books, papers or tools which you have borrowed ;
- and, on your last day, express your feelings of gratitude to the Chef, who has guided you, and the brigade with whom you have worked. In France, it is usual to offer a drink to everyone after the meal service has ended.

You do not need to buy an expensive bottle of wine, but the gesture will be much appreciated.

– 3 –
in
GERMANY
[D]

by
Marianne Müller
Head of the "Hotelfachschule Heidelberg"

Translation by
Jutta Helliwell
and
Professor **Derek C. Gladwell,** OBE
MA, FHCIMA, FRSA

D

GERMANY

Before you leave

If you are considering going to Germany for practical kitchen training, you should be aware that conditions are different from those of your own country.

• As in England, there is no special legal category for a practical training placement (« Praktikum ») and trainees are therefore entitled to normal statutory conditions of service and remuneration, unless a specific agreement (such as that described below) has been negotiated with the employer. (This situation contrasts with that of France, where a traineeship or « stage » is regulated on a different basis from that of ordinary employment).

• Many German firms are willing to take trainees, to help them with their studies. Because the trainees are not experienced or fully qualified, they are usually paid a modest allowance rather than a full wage. This may amount (in 1991 terms) to about 300 DM (German Marks) weekly which is equivalent to about £100 Sterling.

• Making the arrangements for a « praktikum » can be quite lengthy and you should start planning at least six months in advance. This is especially important if you are not a citizen of a country in the European Community.

• If you are taking a sandwich course, you should apply through your College. Otherwise, the normal first step for a UK citizen may be to apply through :

The British Hospitality Association
(BHA, formerly BHRCA)
40 Duke Street, LONDON WIM 6HR
Telephone : 071-499-6641

The scheme run by the BHA on behalf of Hotrec is described on p. 9
Those who are not UK citizens can directly contact the following German bodies :

Zihoga
Feuerbachstr. 42-46
6000 Frankfurt am Main
Telephone : 069-711-0

or :
Dehoga (short for Deutscher Hotel- und Gaststättenverband) Kronprinzenstr. 46
5300 Bonn - Bad Godesberg

OR THE INTERNATIONAL BODY :

HOTREC

Bd Anspach 111, bte 4
1000 Bruxelles, Belgium
Tel. 32 2 513 63 23 - Fax 32 2 513 89 54

Making the application

As soon as you have been put in touch with an employer or Chef, you should make a written application. This should include :

- your curriculum vitae (typewritten) with a photograph ;
- a short letter of application (in your own handwriting) stating why you have chosen to apply to that particular company and the dates when you would be available ;
- copies of any school reports and assessments and of any references you may have from previous jobs or training placements.

Request information from the employer on :

- the nature of the post offered to you, its duration and a proposed starting date ;
- whether accommodation and board will be provided and what remuneration will be paid.

Formal arrangements

Before your departure, give careful thought to all the papers and formalities which may be necessary.

(1) Papers and documents :

- identity card or passport (and parental authorization if you are a minor) ;
- national health insurance documents ;

- the training agreement or employment contract or correspondence with your prospective employer ;
- personal documents, such as your driving licence (if any), a doctor's certificate stating that you can work without risk to your health, and vaccination/immunization records ;
- insurance covering you against claims by third parties and also motor insurance if you are taking a car.

(2) If you are staying for more than three months, you will need an extended residence permit (« Langzeitaufenthaltsgenehmigung »). However, citizens of countries in the European Community are exempt from this requirement.

(3) Clothing : you will need :
- your working clothes ;
- (depending on the time of year) warm, waterproof clothing.

You would also be well advised to obtain as much information as possible about the region and town in which you will be working.

Accidents and Illness

In Germany, employers are required to register employees (even those staying only for a short period) with the « Sozialversicherung » (the health insurance system), so that in case of illness they are covered for treatment.
Employers are responsible for accident insurance and you will therefore be covered for any accident occurring at your place of work.

You yourself must take out insurance to cover the possibility that you might cause an accident to another person. Drivers must take out third party insurance. The necessary insurance arrangements should be made before you leave your own country.

Termination of the work contract (« Praktikum »)

The contract cannot be terminated unless there are very special reasons or circumstances beyond the control of the parties.

Termination by the employee can take place if there is :

- physical assault ;
- intolerable conduct by the employer ;
- a breach of the conditions of employment ;
- non-payment of remuneration.

Termination by the employer can take place if there is :

- physical assault ;
- intolerable conduct by the employee ;
- breach of trust or breach of confidence ;
- refusal by the employee to carry out his/her duties ;
- serious neglect of safety rules.

And now to the kitchen !

You have come to gain experience of German cuisine. This is not as world-famous as French cuisine-indeed, there is no « German cuisine » as such, but there is excellent regional cookery. There are also many first-class Chefs who are highly skilled in both international cuisine and the dishes of their own region.

If you train under a Chef of this kind, your role will probably be that of a Commis within the kitchen brigade. If you want to learn as much as possible during your stay, you should show enthusiasm for your work, accept that many things are not the same as in your own country, and give unstintingly of your time and energy to gain experience. In this way, you will become accepted as a full working member of the brigade.

The kitchen brigade

In all good hotels, the organization of the kitchen brigade is similar to that of the French model. The hierarchy is as follows (French titles tend to be used) :

Management : The Chef (« Küchenchef »)
Sous-Chef (i.e. the deputy chef)

Link between kitchen and restaurant : « Annonceur »

Sections or « Parties » : « Rôtisseur » (Roast Chef)
« Saucier » (Sauce Chef)
« Gardemanger » (Larder Chef)
« Entremétier » (responsible for vegetables and entrées)
« Poissonnier » (Fish Chef).
« Pâtissier » (Pastry Chef).

These Sections each have their specialist functions and are complemented by the « Tournant » (Relief Chef), « Regimier » (Diet Chef) and « Communard » (Staff Chef) ; there is also the « Glacier » (ice cream specialist), « Confiseur » (Confectioner) and « Boulanger » (Baker). In addition, there are the « Commis » (junior cooks), the apprentices, the trainees, and the washing-up staff and kitchen porters.

The Chef has total responsibility for organization, production, efficient use of resources, and staff training :
- he allocates tasks and arranges the daily working schedules and rotas ;
- he appoints the staff and ensures that they receive training and opportunities for personal development;
- he decides upon the quality and quantity of goods purchased ;
- he draws up the kitchen budget and is responsible for the financial results ;
- he plans the menus, ensures uniform standards of quality and encourages creativity.

The Roast Chef is responsible for all roasts and for dishes prepared in fat or oil : these are mainly meat dishes, but also include chicken, turkey, game, fish and vegetables. When necessary, he is supported by a specialist Grill Chef, who usually works in full view of the customers and may use a charcoal grill.

The Sauce Chef prepares sauces, sauce-based dishes (such as ragouts) and dishes which are cooked in a frying pan. He also prepares fish dishes, if there is no separate Fish Chef. More often than not, he is also the Sous-Chef.

The Larder Chef and his assistants prepare the cold dishes, cold sauces, salads and cold garnishes ; they have a special responsibility for cold buffets. The Larder Chef is in charge of the refrigerated storage of foods and of cutting up meat and preparing poultry. He may be assisted by a Butcher (in German, « Metzger) and/or an Hors d'œuvre Chef (« Vorspeisenkoch »).

The Entremétier is responsible for : soups ; vegetables and vegetable garnishes (except those which are grilled or fried) ; potato, rice and pasta dishes ; and hot hors d'œuvre and egg dishes. He deals with dietary requirements when there is no Diet Chef and with pastry and sweet dishes when there is no Pastry Chef.

The Pastry Chef is responsible for confectionery, sweet dishes, desserts and sweet garnishes. His role is wider than that of his counterpart in a shop. Apart from pastry, « petits fours », cakes and baked goods, he produces ices, pastry for other sections of the kitchen, and small savouries. The range of responsibilities of his section depends upon the size of the establishment. He may be assisted by a Baker, a sugarwork specialist (for small confectionery and sugar products, eg, pralines) and/or an ice cream specialist.

The Fish Chef deals with all fish dishes (except grilled and fried dishes) and their related garnishes, together with fish soups and fish sauces. He is also in charge of the storage and preparation of shellfish and crustaceans.

Supporting the primary and secondary sections are : the **Relief Chef,** who deputises in the absence of the Section Chefs (« Chefs de partie ») and the **Staff Chef** who, with the assistance of the junior staff, produces the staff meals.

Working Practices

You should be aware of the working practices in Germany.

- Staff normally work 38-42 hours per week, with two days off ; the normal working day is 8 hours, with the possibility of up to 11 hours when necessary. Some establishments work split shifts, whilst others have straight shifts.

- Punctuality is a key requirement : this is especially important in a kitchen, because the customers cannot be kept waiting.

- No smoking is allowed in kitchens.

- Personal hygiene is a top priority and you should always wear correct dress (chef's hat, jacket, trousers, neckerchief, apron and kitchen rubber).

- It is very important that you should keep your working area tidy, well-organized and clean.

In every country, some kitchens are equipped with modern appliances and some are less modern. Every kitchen naturally has freezer and refrigeration equipment and an increasing number have induction hobs, convection ovens and the « Sous-vide » system.

The food hygiene laws are important and are very strict and complex. In Germany, a cook has to obey up to 150 regulations affecting his work. He must be aware of all hygiene and safety requirements including, for example, those concerned with minced meat, duck eggs, ice cream and the handling of meat. You should ask for the more important regulations to be explained to you.

- You will notice differences in the overall approach to cooking. For example, although classical cooking is based on the French model, it is modified in Germany to become lighter in character. German regional dishes have rules which are all their own !

Make the best of your stay

You will want to make the best use of both your job opportunity and your personal time whilst you are in Germany.

You will find that it is just as important to listen, watch and practise as it is to read and make notes. It is, nevertheless, helpful to make notes about anything unusual or interesting - and to ask for more information if you are not clear on any point.

It is important, for the sake of your career development, to be inquisitive. Try to do and to see as much as possible. Your questions will be gladly answered. If you want to widen your experience by working in other parts of the kitchen, ask to be transferred.

German eating habits

Breakfast, the midday meal and the evening meal have traditionally been eaten by all the members of the family together. However, this has become less common, because many people work shifts or have a long journey between their home and their work. There is a trend towards lighter and healthier meals, due in part to the change in habits arising from the increase in sedentary work.

Breakfast is taken between 6.00 am and 8.00 am, depending on individual hours of work. It may be either a light or a substantial meal. It always includes coffee (with milk), bread or bread rolls, butter and jam. Some people also have fruit juice, eggs, German sausage and cheese, whilst others prefer cornflakes, soft cheese, yoghurt and fruit.

The midday meal is taken between 12.00 noon and 1.30 pm. This used to be regarded as a family meal and consisted of soup, a main course and dessert. Pressure of work has changed most people's habits and many now eat in their firm's canteen. Full 3-course meals are available in canteens, although lighter meals are usually preferred - and sometimes just a snack or salad. People usually drink water or, less often, beer ; wine is rarely drunk at this meal.

The evening meal is usually taken between 6.00 pm and 8.00 pm, although the time varies considerably from one region to another. Those who have had a hot meal at midday would normally have a cold collation, such as bread and butter with sliced sausage and cheese, accompanied by tea, beer or wine. Those who have had a cold snack at midday would have a hot meal in the evening. When the meal is at a restaurant - for example, a business meal or a special occasion with family or friends - the classic choice would be several courses and two accompanying wines. The gourmet restaurants have helped in recent years to revive this classic tradition.

Each region in Germany has its distinctive style of cooking, based on farmhouse traditions and using local products.

• In the North (Schleswig-Holstein and Niedersachsen), fresh fish and other seafood from the North Sea are important. The countryside produces an abundance of fruit and this has led to the development of specialities such as « Rote Krütze » (a deep red jelly made from mixed red and dark berries). Like many other North Europeans, the people of this area are fond of sweet foods ; specialities include a sweet-sour soup. If they drink wine, it is usually a medium sweet type, but many prefer beer.

• In central Germany (Hessen and Nordrhein-Westfalen), the Eastern area is less prosperous than the Western. In the latter, especially near the Rhine, you can find every type of vegetable and very good wines. The style of cooking is richer than in the North and has been influenced by the cuisine of neighbouring countries. There are exciting specialities, such as Bergische Coffee.

• In the South, the area surrounding the River Main (Baden-Württemberg and Bavaria) is rich in agricultural products and has some of the best wines. Bavarian cooking tends to be heavy and is well-known for dishes such as sauerkraut (incidentally, it is not true that all Germans eat sauerkraut !), knuckle of pork (« Schweinehaxen »), dumplings, large white radishes (« Radi ») and beer. The cuisine of Baden-Württemberg is more complex. The traditional cookery of Baden is complemented by Swabian specialities, such as « Schupfnudeln » (a pasta of semolina or flour with eggs), « Maultaschen » (a special type of meat pasty) and « Rostbrätle » (a sort of roast beef). Because it has the longest border with France, this area has been influenced by French cuisine.

Types of dining places

All establishments serving food and beverages to be consumed on the premises are called « restaurants ».

You can find :

(1) Restaurants, which specialize in better-class meals and may be either free standing or part of a hotel. The best restaurants are those which have the highest qualified Chefs (« Sterneköche ») and these are the most suitable for training. Most themed restaurants, such as French restaurants, belong to this group.

(2) Fast food and snack bars.

(3) Motorway service areas.

(4) Restaurants at railway stations

(5) Eating places of foreign origin, which have taken root in Germany, such as pizzerias.

General information

You will want to make the best use of your free time. The German countryside is very beautiful, with many places of interest. Your local Tourist Information Office will be able to advise you on museums, monuments and other places to visit in the town itself and the surrounding area.

You will find the following information useful :

• In towns, the Post Offices are open from 9.00 am to 5.00 pm from Mondays to Fridays and 9.00 am to 11.00 am or 9.00 am to 12.00 noon on Saturdays. Major cities may have a late-closing counter (« Nachtschalter »)

• For long-distance telephone calls, dial the code for the country usually after beginning with 00. It is not necessary to wait for a dialling tone.

• Opening hours for banks are 8.00 am to 4.00 pm from Mondays to Fridays, with late opening until 6.00 pm on Thursdays.

• Opening hours for shops are 9.00 am to 6.00 pm from Mondays to Fridays, with late opening until 8.30 pm on Thursdays. On Saturdays, they close at 12.00 noon, except on the first Saturday of every month, which is known as « long Saturday » (« langen Samstage »). In some of the major departmental stores, it is well worthwhile to visit the grocery and wine sections.

Hotel and catering training in Germany

It will be of interest to you to know how your colleagues at work have been trained.
Full-time courses at College, which are normal in other European countries, have no counterpart in Germany. Instead, training is based on a dual system and takes place partly in College and partly at work. The training contract is therefore between the employer and the apprentice (« Lehrling ») and lasts for three years. During this period, the apprentice works in the business and attends College either on two days a week or on a block-release basis. At the end of the training period, the apprentice takes an examination in his/her specialism (eg, as a cook) : this examination is conducted by the IHK and is known as the « Gehilfenprüfung ». On passing this examination, he/she becomes a qualified cook and can be employed as a Commis.

Before returning home

As your training period draws to an end, you should make sure that you have extracted the maximum benefit from your stay. Look through your notes and do not hesitate to ask questions - your Chef will be very willing to advise you.

To help you keep in touch with what is happening in German hotels and restaurants, the following addresses may be useful :

(a) Trade journals :
« Hotel Restaurant » (monthly)
published by : Matthaes Verlag, Olgastr. 87, 7000 Stuttgart.
Küche » (monthly) and « Maitre » (6 issues per year) both published by :
Rhenania Fachverlag, Schumannstr. 27, 6000 Frankfurt.

(b) Guides :
The best-known international gastronomic guides are those of Michelin and Gault-Millau, but there are also many others.

(c) Trade Exhibitions :
There are exhibitions in every region, taking place on various dates during the year. The best known are the ITB in Berlin and the special gastronomic trade fairs in Hannover, Cologne, Frankfurt, Stuttgart and Munich.

(d) Books :
There are a great many books available, amongst the most important for cooks being :
Hering : « Lexikon der Küche »
and
Pauli : « Lehrbuch der Küche »
Apart from the above, there is such a wide choice that it is advisable to send for the full lists from the leading publishers :

- Hugo Matthaes Verlag
Olgastr. 87, 7000 Stuttgart

- Falkenverlag
Schöne Aussicht 21, 6272 Niedernhausen.

• Finally, when you are getting ready to leave, remember to :

- ask your employer for your certificate or a report ;

- return all books and property which you may have borrowed ;

- and thank the Manager, the Chef and all those with whom you have worked.

— 4 —

in

SPAIN
[SP]

by
J.M. Jaen Avila
Director
''Sol'' Tourism College, Madrid

Translation by
Maria Urdiales

and

Professor **Derek C. Gladwell,** OBE
MA, FHCIMA, FRSA

Before you leave

Practical training in Spain

The idea of practical training as a complement to hotel school education has evolved in Spain alongside the growth in tourism.

In the early days, training took place in restaurants (especially hotel restaurants) under the supervision of competent professionals. It received the full backing of the managers, who recognized the importance of practical training for hotel students.

However, the ever-increasing number of tourists led to the employment of inexperienced staff and this led to a decline in the standard of customer service. The situation was such that many staff lacked even the basic elements of professional skills. It was therefore decided to seek the support of the technical colleges in an effort to increase the number of competent staff available.

There is now a more satisfactory balance between supply and demand, but simultaneously the clientele is demanding better value for money through improved quality of service. Firms are therefore having to select staff with appropriate qualifications, who can work to the required standards.

Government regulations relating to practical training

Requirements prior to undertaking a traineeship or employment in Spain

For students from hotel schools in countries which have a reciprocal agreement with Spain, there is a system of mutual recognition operated by the Spanish Ministry of Labour and Social Security.

If you want to make your training arrangements independently, you can apply to :

1 - any hotel chain with establishments in the various regions of Spain ; or

2 - any restaurant listed in the Michelin, Campsa or similar guides. You should include in your application a typewritten curriculum vitae (the original and a photocopy) and state clearly the type of training you are seeking, a proposed starting date and duration, and any requests you may wish to make concerning accommodation, the provision of staff meals, and remuneration.

Documentation

In making your preparations for leaving for Spain, you should be aware of the documents required under the arrangements agreed within the European Community (EC.) These vary according to which of the following groups you fall into :

A - Non-Spanish students undertaking practical training ("trainees") ;

B - Non-Spanish employees.

A - For the first category (non-Spanish students undertaking practical training) the following documents are required :

1 - An application for permission to undertake the training, including the proposed length of your stay in Spain (include also a photocopy of this document).

2 - A photocopy of your current passport, attested by the Spanish Consulate in your own country.

3 - An application for a visa to be issued by the Spanish Consulate in your own country.

4 - A certificate showing that you have had no criminal convictions in your own country (or a suitable substitute document).

5 - A medical certificate.

6 - A certificate that you are a student or that you have had on-the - job training and that the proposed practical training is an integral part of your studies.

7 - A training contract from your proposed employer or a letter confirming that a training contract will be entered into.

8 - In addition, you will find it useful to carry your Student Union card (if you have one).

At the present time, the following four countries have a formal training agreement with Spain : Switzerland, France, Germany and Italy. Each of these has its own local office to handle the required documentation, the

addresses being as follows :

Switzerland : Office Fédéral de l'Industrie, des Arts et Métiers et du Travail (OFIAMT).
Division de la Main d'Œuvre et de l'Emigration
Bundesgasse, 8, 3003 Bern, Switzerland

France : Office des Migrations Internationales (OMI)
Calle Recoletos, 19-3° Dcha
28001 Madrid, Spain

Germany : Bundesanstalt fur Arbeitsvermittlung und Arbeitlosenversicherung
Zentralstelle fur Arbeitsvermittlung
Feuerbachstrasse 42-46,
6000 Frankfurt/main, 1, Germany

Italy : Ministerio de Trabajo y Previsión Social
Roma, Italy

The office for correspondence in Spain is :
Instituto Español de Emigracion
Calle Pintor Rosales, 46
28008 Madrid
Telephone : 91/247.52.00

In the case of countries (at the time of writing, including the UK) which do not have a formal training agreement with Spain, it is necessary, in addition to the above documents, for the receiving firm to show that there will be an exchange of trainees.

In both cases, the maximum duration of a traineeship in Spain is 12 months, with 6 months extension.

B - for the second category (non-Spanish employees) the following steps should be taken :

1 - Make an application for a visa to be issued by the Spanish Consulate in your own country.

2 - Obtain a preliminary offer of employment from the Spanish firm offering the work.

3 - When you have obtained proof that you have applied for the visa, the rest of the documents should be sent to :

Direccion Provincial de Trabajo
Calle Cristimo Martos, 4
28015 Madrid
Telephone : 91/248.44.00

These documents comprise :

a - Proof that you have applied for the visa.

b - A medical certificate.

o A certificate showing that you have had no criminal convictions in your own country (or a suitable substitute document).

d - Forms TC1 and TC2 relating to your last month with your firm.

e - A record of your employment with your firm.

f - A clear statement of the kind of work you intend to undertake.

g - A note of your next of kin, in case of accident.

h - If a specific qualification is required, evidence for the Spanish Ministry of Education and Science that you hold such a qualification.

You have to obtain an identity card for staying in Spain and this is available for the same length of time as your contract of employment a maximum : of 5 years with automatic renewal.

When a contract of employment is for less than 3 months, it is only necessary to have a simple form of authorization ("autorizacion de trabajo"). When it exceeds this length, you must apply for a work permit ("permiso de trabajo") : this is renewable if your firm wishes to extend your contract.

Insurance requirements

• Trainees

In accordance with existing national agreements wthin the European Community, trainees enjoy the same health and Social Security benefits (including medical and hospital facilities) as their counterparts in Spain, provided that they have been members of their own national insurance scheme. For this purpose, they should retain the receipt for the college fees paid in their own country.

Before leaving Britain, you should tell your local Social Security Office that you will be undertaking a traineeship in Spain and obtain the appropriate Form 111. This is the form that you will have to produce in order to get free medical treatment in Spain, if you have an accident or illness.

It is advisable to carry with you the original and photocopies of form 111 and also of your college fees receipt. However, always retain the originals and, when you have to produce one of these forms, hand over only a photocopy.

If a problem arises whilst in Spain, due to illness, accident or other misfortune, you should immediately take or send photocopies of these documents to the following offices :

Instituto de la Seguridad Social
Calle Dr Gómez Ulla, 2-1°, Madrid
Telephone : 256 45 00

and
Instituto de la Seguridad Social
(Student Security Section)
Calle Velázquez, 105-1°, Madrid
Telephone : 564 27 38

The latter is the administrative centre for all Social Security matters relating to **students** (Spanish or foreign) enrolled in any Spanish college (if they are between 14 and 28 years of age), provided that both they and their college are within the Social Security system.

You can also get information from :
OMI
Calle Recoletos 19
28001 Madrid
Telephone : 575 12 44

• Employees

Non-Spanish **employees** ought to apply to be enrolled in the Social Security system **before leaving their own country.** The relevant forms are :

- ''Impreso'' 101
- ''Impreso'' 106 or 111 (one or other of these two)

When these forms have been authenticated, they will serve as your medical card in case you need medical assistance. It is advisable, as with the forms previously mentioned, to carry photocopies, so that you can always retain the originals.

The administrative centre for Social Security matters

relating to foreign **employees** is (as already referred to) :

Instituto de la Seguridad Social
Calle Dr Gomez Ulla, 2
Madrid
Telephone : 256 45 00

Further information can also be obtained from OMI (as above).

The medical assistance is automatically free and the same as that available to any Spanish employee within the Social Security system.

An overview of the restaurant sector in Spain

The restaurant sector is in the midst of major changes and is having to adapt its production techniques so that they are more compatible with the demands of the weather, especially the high temperatures. The following is an overview of recent developments :

Quick-service catering outlets (such as bars, cafeterias and taverns) have tended to have weaknesses in their organization structure and to be lacking in equipment, especially refrigeration.

They are now developing themselves into more-clearly-defined fast food restaurants, such as, for example, sandwich bars, omelette bars, ham bars or fried fish shops. This is leading to an improvement both in their products and in their image.

Classical restaurants in hotels, although managed by skilled professional restaurateurs, suffer in about 30% of cases from poor marketing and obsolete equipment. Many are now increasing their banqueting trade and thus contributing to the full exploitation of the hotel's potential.

Even classical restaurants which have held leading positions for up to 40 years, have benefited considerably by the influence of French methods in the development of their production and service techniques.

There is a growth in the **of number new-style restaurants,** with up-to-date equipment and staff who are well-qualified in kitchen and dining room work.

These are able to maintain good standards and their menus are designed to reflect the customer's needs as well as varying according to the season.

During your training

Kitchen equipment

Over the past ten years, the restaurant industry has had to re-assess its operational methods and reduce labour costs by the use of more labour-saving equipment. Staff have had to learn to accept a competitive environment and be retrained in new methods both in the kitchen itself and in the ancillary areas of work.

You should keep this situation in mind when you examine the equipment in Spanish restaurants. These fall broadly into two categories.

First-class restaurants with modern equipment

Generally speaking, the situation is as described in the previous section, although the actual equipment requirements of individual establishments depend on :
- the location of the restaurant ;
- the type of menus served ;
- the extent to which the restaurant specializes in order to cut labour costs.

The adoption of new technology makes it possible to introduce major changes in working methods : fewer staff are needed, although they have to be more skilled, and the more sophisticated production methods lead to a higher volume of production. It has to be remembered, however, that the choice of dishes may not be as extensive and the customers may not get as much individual attention.

The Spanish approach to fast food, as offered in taverns, bars, etc.

In the large cities, mini-kitchens are being squeezed into every available space in this type of establish ment. They usually have two counters, containing high-output equipment, and have a large turnover of fast food. Space in these kitchens is at a premium and has to be fully utilized.

The main items of equipment are usually :

- high-performance cookers ;
- fry tops ;
- salamanders ;
- fryers ;
- pressure cookers.

The kitchen brigade

The kitchen brigade (ie, the group of kitchen staff responsible for producing meals) consists of the following personnel :

The Head Chef, who is in charge of the kitchen. He receives instructions and advice from the General Manager and has a wide range of responsibilities :

- engaging and dismissing staff ;
- deciding on hours of work, days off and holidays ;
- supervising the work of the staff ;
- being responsible for the kitchen premises and equipment ;
- controlling expenditure ;
- purchasing supplies and checking on their quality and yield ;
- fixing the prices of the table d'hôte and à la carte menus ;
- carrying out regular stocktakings ;
- allocating duties between the kitchen staff.

The Sous-Chef (Deputy Chef)

- replaces the Head Chef in his absence ;
- supervises the work of the brigade ;
- gives support to sections which have an excessive workload ;
- during meal times, takes charge at the waiters' service point.

Chefs de Partie (Section Chefs)

Each chef de partie is responsible to the Head Chef for the work of his section. Their fields of responsibility vary according to circumstances.

• *Sauce Chef*

- deputises for the Head Chef if there is no Sous-Chef ;
- prepares warm sauces, fish (except if fried or grilled), warm shellfish dishes, meat dishes (except if
  roast or grilled) and most other warm main and side
  dishes.

• *Roast and Grill Chef*

- does the roasting and frying ; grills meat and fish.

• *The Chef Entremétier*

- cooks vegetables and vegetable garnishes, potatoes (except if fried), egg dishes, pasta and farina-
  ceous dishes.

• *The Fish Chef*

- cooks fish dishes.

• *The Soup Chef*

- produces soups, consommés, etc.

• *Larder Chef*

- in charge of the cold room with the following staff :

  Butcher   - prepares meat
  Fishmonger   - prepares fish
  Hors d'Œuvre Chef - prepares cold hors d'œuvre
  Buffet Chef - decorates, carves and serves
  buffets

• *The Pastry Chef*

- prepares hot and cold sweets and confectionery. He
  has an assistant who looks after the utensils, does
  the portering jobs, collects requisitioned goods from
  the stores, and does any other work requested by
  the pastry chef.

• *The Staff Cook*

- prepares the meals of the kitchen brigade, etc.

• *Kitchen Porters*

- potato peeling, table scrubbing, lighting the cookers,
  cleaning, etc.

• *Potmen*

- washing pots and pans.

• Cleaning Staff

- kitchen cleaning.

Brigade for a large kitchen

```
                    Jefe de cocina
                         │
                         │
                  SOUS-CHEF
                  2e Jefe de cocina
                         │
   ┌─────────┬───────────┼───────────┬─────────────┬──────────┐
   │         │           │           │             │          │
SAUCE CHEF  CHEF-     LARDER CHEF  PASTRY CHEF  STAFF COOK
Jefe Salsero ENTREMETIER (COLD ROOM) Jefe Pastelero Familiar
                      Jefe cuartofrio
```

SAUCE CHEF — Jefe Salsero
- Roast Chef
- Gril Chef
- Sauces Section
- 1st & 2nd Assistants

CHEF-ENTREMETIER
- Entremets Section
- Fish Chef
- Soup Chef
- 1st & 2nd Assistants

LARDER CHEF (COLD ROOM) — Jefe cuartofrio
- Butcher
- Fishmonger
- Hors d'Ouvre Chef
- Buffet Chef
- 1st & 2nd Assistants

PASTRY CHEF — Jefe Pastelero
- Pastry Section
- 1st & 2nd Assistants

STAFF COOK — Familiar

KITCHEN PORTERS — Pinche

POTMEN — Marmiton

KITCHEN CLEANERS — Personal de Limpieza

SP

Spanish eating habits

There are very noticeable differences between the eating habits of Spain and those of the rest of the European Community, both in the way food is prepared and in the times of meals.

These habits are, however, slowly beginning to change, due to the fact that many (although still a minority) of the city workers are no longer eating their main meal at home, which is where traditional habits are most tenaciously maintained.

• Generally speaking, the Spanish eat a great deal of pulses, potatoes, rice and green vegetables, together with fresh fruit and salads (mainly of tomatoes and lettuce, which are abundant throughout Spain).

The most commonly used meats, at home and in restaurants, are beef, lamb and pork, preferably fresh rather than frozen.

The tradition with pork and pork products is that they are not merely processed to prolong their shelf life but rather they are carefully cured and treated in order to increase their value : ham, dried loin of pork, special hard sausages and Spanish black pudding are all marketed at high prices because of their excellent quality. Although there is a great variety of blood sausages and other pork specialities - such as a stew with pigs snout and ears and a dish made with fried fat from streaky bacon - pork is not eaten as much as it was previously, as it has partly been replaced by beef and lamb, in order to reduce the amount of saturated fat in the diet.

Fatty snacks in general are being replaced by "tapas", the famous and infinitely-varied tit-bits which are offered in bars and restaurants, alongside other dishes such as those using offal or brain.

Fish and shellfish are available in a wide variety of delicious dishes not only in the coastal regions, where they are particularly plentiful, but also in inland areas, although in the latter there is less choice. The Spanish avoid frozen fish as often as their budget permits, although at family level they often nowadays have to accept the frozen variety because it is cheaper.

Eggs and pasta dishes form an increasing part of the diet of the middle classes.

The flavour of many oven-cooked and fried foods owes much to the use of olive oil, which is graded, according to taste and custom, on the basis of its acidity and degree of refinement. In general, in roasts (but only in roasts) pork fat is used instead of olive oil.

Spanish food is usually highly flavoured as plenty of garlic, onion and spices are used in the main traditional dishes.

People prefer bread made with white flour, although small quantities of brown bread are consumed. Bread is an essential part of all meals.

• The main meals are breakfast, lunch and supper. Portions at lunch and supper tend to be bigger than in other European countries.

Breakfast taken at home is normally a very light meal, consisting of a drink of milk or coffee and either a small piece of sweet cake or biscuits or bread, with or without butter. In a cafe, the traditional way of taking coffee is with "churros" (thin rings of fried pastry sprinkled with sugar).

Country people have a heavier breakfast to provide energy and to ward off the cold of the early morning frost. This would include eggs with breadcrumbs, "sopas de ajo" (a heavy dish of bread, streaky bacon, eggs, garlic and pimiento), eggs with bacon and so on, accompanied by wine.

Hotels are now introducing the buffet breakfast, with an international choice of dishes.

Lunch ("almuerzo") is the main meal of the day - and the main supplier of calories ! It is a big meal, taken between 2.00 pm and 3.30 pm, and consists of three courses - a starter, main dish and sweet.

Popular dishes include hot soup in winter and "gazpachos" (a cold soup) in summer.

Many families drink red wine with their meals and the soporific effect of this (especially in the humid heat of summer) makes the afternoon "siesta" (period of rest) essential.

Supper ("cena"), the last meal of the day, is rather lighter and is not usually taken before 10.00 pm. In recent times, it has changed from being a cooked meal to one which consists of simpler dishes such as cold meat, sausage, eggs, cheese, fruit, salad and milk, with plenty of fried potatoes when the house-wife is in a good mood !

Respect for meal times is a strictly-required act of courtesy. Similarly, in bars they keep to set times for the service of ''tapas'' and for the service of beers and wines. Some people may find this a little strange, but it must be remembered that, in Spain, bars are like clubs, where people meet friends, business associates and acquaintances.

Older people normally have a high tea (''merienda'') in the middle of the afternoon, instead of supper - but children have both high tea and supper if they are awake until late in the evening, as usually happens in summer !

Nevertheless, in the bigger towns, where the rhythm of life is governed by working hours, traffic and shortage of time, a daily routine like that of other European countries is gradually being more widely adopted ; in addition, dietary habits are being simplified and meals are increasingly being eaten outside the home.

Spanish regional cuisine

If you know the region, you will know the style of cooking. The culinary art of each region is based on local custom and its development has been influenced by the pattern of daily life, the climate and the types of food most readily available. Each region has its own recipes and ingredients. In the case of a dish such as ''Bacalao Ajoarriero'' (dried salted cod cooked and flavoured with garlic), we shall never know in which region it originated, but individual versions are highly regarded in Navarre, Castile Léon, Castile La Mancha, and even in Aragon. Likewise, we find other dishes which, although similarly named, are totally different in different parts of the country.

Everyone has heard of ''Paella Valenciana'' (made from rice, shellfish, chicken and vegetables), but there is also a great variety of other specialized dishes - and utensils - all with a uniquely Spanish character. Here are a few examples : ''Potes'' (cooking pots on legs) in Galicia and Asturias ; ''Zarzuelas'' (a dish of mixed fish in a pimiento sauce) and ''Escalibadas'' (meat cooked barbecue-style) in Catalonia ; ''Parrilladas'' and "Pil-piles" (distinctive types of grill) in the Basque country ; unique roast dishes in Castile ; "Chilindrones" (stews with various meats) in Aragon ; fried dishes in Andalucia ; corn soup and "gofio" (a kind of porridge) in the Canary Islands ; "Calderetas" (lamb prepared in a sauce, similar to a stew) in Estremadura ; and special stews in Majorca and the Balearic Islands.

In short, with the regional differences and the distinctive way in which food is prepared and cooked, you will find that Spain has an attractive variety of cuisine.

Hotel and catering training

The following paragraphs summarize the areas of knowledge considered necessary in the main managerial and departmental posts in Spanish hotels and restaurants.

Hotel general manager (in charge of the hotel)

Compulsory aspects : technical knowledge of tourist activities and business.

Supporting studies : technical knowledge and skills in the kitchen, guest services and buildings maintenance ;
economics and entrepreneurial skills ;
law ;
information technology ;
training in management skills.

Reception department

Compulsory aspects : none
Professional knowledge : technical knowledge relating to tourist activities and business ;
advance reservations and reception operations ;
certificates in foreign languages ;
technical business knowledge ;
information technology ;
a single-subject course ;
training in management skills.

Food and beverage department

• Kitchen area
Compulsory aspects : none
Professional knowledge : specialist kitchen techniques ;
a single-subject course ;
practical skills development.

• Service Area
Compulsory aspects : none
Professional knowledge : specialist service techniques ;
a single-subject course ;
training in foreign languages ;
practical skills development ;
specialized training in wines (or a similar speciality).

Housekeeping department

Compulsory aspects : none
Professional knowledge : specialist techniques for
maintaining and cleaning the accommodation area ;
a single-subject course ;
practical skills development to a high standard.

Educational routes into hotel and tourism education

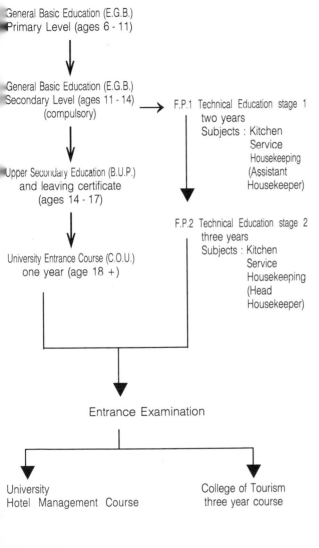

General Basic Education (E.G.B.)
Primary Level (ages 6 - 11)

General Basic Education (E.G.B.)
Secondary Level (ages 11 - 14)
(compulsory)

F.P.1 Technical Education stage 1
two years
Subjects : Kitchen
Service
Housekeeping
(Assistant
Housekeeper)

Upper Secondary Education (B.U.P.)
and leaving certificate
(ages 14 - 17)

F.P.2 Technical Education stage 2
three years
Subjects : Kitchen
Service
Housekeeping
(Head
Housekeeper)

University Entrance Course (C.O.U.)
one year (age 18 +)

Entrance Examination

University
Hotel Management Course

College of Tourism
three year course

Abbreviations

E.G.B. = Educación General Basica
B.U.P. = Bachillerato Unificado y Polivalente
C.O.U. = Curso de Orientación Universitaria
F.P. = Formación Profesional

SP

Before you return home

The best things to buy in Spain

Those who know Spain well are in a position to know the best things to buy, either because they are exclusive or because they combine good quality with a moderate price.

The following information on products which are characteristic of Spain may help you to choose some souvenirs.

Pottery is one of the best-known Spanish crafts : every region has its own distinctive clay, colouring and decorative style. Equally important is the beautiful embroidery from centres such as the Canary Islands, Lagartera and Segovia... or the blonde lace with which they make the famous Spanish mantillas (headdresses).

Leather, embossed work, wrought iron, Toledo metal craftsmanship, copper and bronze work, glasswork gilded in silver, and a typical style of fan are other goods which deserve a mention for their fine craftsmanship.

For porcelain, it is important to mention Lladro, which is world famous for its unique and delicate designs.

Articles made from skins - suede or leather - are of excellent quality and very well finished : for example, harnesses and other riding equipment.

If you go to Majorca, you will find the well-known cultured pearls known as ''Majórica'' - and these can also be found in jewellers' shops in other cities.

Important amongst the distinctive Spanish food products is the range of sweets, which vary according to the region and the time of year, and the special confections which celebrate festive and saint's days.

Do not forget the cheeses and hams, which have been prepared with such skill that they can satisfy the most refined tastes. Many of them have an official Certificate of Origin and are recognized as being of world-class quality.

There is a wide variety wines - such as Rioja, sherry and Cavas Catalanes - and spirits (including aniseed-based drinks) which are held in high esteem.

A final word of advice is that you should take your time looking round the chops and consult local people, who will tell you where you can get the best bargains. When you buy in a hurry and use tourist shops, you usually pay more and do not always get the best quality.

TRABAJADORES EN PRACTICAS

ESPAÑA

Solicitud de autorización para realizar prácticas profesionales, y para estancia o residencia en España
Antrag auf Bewilligung eines Beruf spraktikums und Aufenhalts-oder Wohnnitzgenehmigung für Spanien
Demande d'autorisation en vue d'effectuer des stages professionnels et pour un séjour ou une résidence temporaire en Espagne
Application for permission to carry out professional training and for temporary or permanent residence in Spain
Richiesta di autorizzazione per formazione professionale, e per soggiorno o residenza in Spagna

NUMERO DE IDENTIFICACION

1

Completar en cuatro ejemplares en letra de imprenta. Marcar con una cruz la respuesta ☒
In Druckschrift vierfach ausfüllen. Die Antwort ankreuzen ☒
A remplir en quatre exemplaires en lettres d'imprimerie. Marquer d'une croix la réponse ☒
Please complete in quadruplicate. Please print. Indicate your answer with an X ☒
Compilare n quatro copie in stampatello. Barrare la risposta ☒

Destino de los ejemplares
1. Dirección Gral. del I. E. Emigración
2. Dirección Gral. Policía (C. Gral. Documentación)
3. Para devolución a D.G.I.E.E. con NIE asignado
4. Para el interesado

| Apellidos / Familienname / Nom / Surname / Cognomi | Fecha de nacimiento / Geburtsdatum / Date de naissance / Date of birth / Data di nascita: | día / mes / año ☐ 1 9 ☐ |
| | En / Geburtsort / Lieu de naisance / Place of birth / Luogo: | |

Nombre / Vorname / Prénoms / First names / Nome	Nacionalidad actual / Nationalität / Nationalité / Nationality / Nazionalità	soltero / ledig / célibataire / single / celibe ☐ 1
		casado / verheiratet / marié / married / coniugato ☐ 2
		otros / sonstige / autres / others / altro ☐ 3
		hombre / männl / homme / male / maschio ☐ 1
		mujer / weibl / femme / female / femmina ☐ 2

Domicilio actual para correspondencia
Für eventuelle Korrespondenz bitte derzeitigen Wohnsitz angeben
Domicile actuel pour adresser la correspondance
Present postal address
Domicilio attuale per recapito corrispondenza

Formación / Ausbildung / Formation / Training / Formazione

| Especialidad / Fach / Spécialisation / Particular field of study / Specializzazione | Número de años / Dauer der Ausbildungszeit / Nombre d'années consacrées / Number of years / Numeri di anni |

Instituciones: ascuelas profesionales, universidades, experiencia profesional / Ausbildungsstätten, Berufsschule, Universität, berufliche Erfahrung /
Institutions: écoles professionnelles, universités, expérience professionnelle / Institutes business schools, universités, professional experience /
Istituzioni: scuole professionali, università, esperienza professionale.

76

Muttersprache
Langue maternelle
Mother tongue
Lingua madre

Autres langues
Other languages
Altre lingue

Empleo actual/Derzeitige Tätigkeit/Emploi actuel/ Present employment/Occupazione attuale	Función/Aufgaben/Fontion/ Duties/Mansioni	Desde/seit/Depuis le/ Date of commencement/dal dia / mes / año
		1 9

Empleos anteriores (también en el extranjero)/Vorherige Beschäftigungen/Emplois anterieurs/Previous employment/Precedenti occupazioni:

Empleador y sector/Arbeitgeber und Abteilung/Employeur et secteur/ Name of employer and type of work/Datore di lavoro e settore	Función/Aufgaben/ Fonction/Duties / Mansioni	Desde-hasta/Von-bis/ Depuis le-jusqu'au/from-to/ Dal-al

Otras estancias en el extranjero/Weitere Auslandsaufenthalte/Autres sejours à l'étranger/Other periods abroad/Altri soggiorni all'estero

Otros conocimientos/Sonstige Kenntnisse/Autres connaissances/Other relevant experience/Altre conoscenze

Taquigrafía-mecanografía/Stenographie. Schreibmaschinenkenntnisse/ Sténographie-dactylographie/Shorthand. Typing/ Stenografia-dattilografia ☐	Permiso de conducir/Führerschein / Driving license/Permis de conduire / Patente auto ☐

Familiares a cargo del trabajador / Unterhaltsberechtigte: Familien- und Vorname, Verwandtschaftsverhältnis, Geburtsdatum / **Famille du travailleur:** Nom et prenom, Parenté, Date de naisance. / **Dependents:** Surname and forename(s), relationship, date of birth. / **Familiari a carico del lavoratore:** Cognome e nome, Relazione di parentela, Data di nascita.

Apellidos y Nombre	Parentesco	Fecha de nacimiento	N.I.E.

Empleo en prácticas / Arbeitsstätte / Emploi (stage) / Employment / Occupazione:

Nombre y dirección del empleador
Name und Anschrift des Arbeitgebers
Nom et adresse de l'employeur
Name and address of employer
Nome e indirizzo del datore di lavoro:

Puesto de trabajo
Arbeitsplatz
Poste de travail
Position held
Posto di lavoro

Salario bruto
Bruttogehalt
Salaire brut
Gross salary
Retribuzione lorda

Fecha de incorporación
Beginn des Arbeitsverhältnisses
Date de la prise de fonctions
Date of commencement
Data di inizio del lavoro

Duración del empleo (máx. 1 año)
Dauer des Arbeitsverhältnisses (max. 1 jahr)
Durée de l'emploi (max. 1 année)
Period of employment (max. 1 year)
Durata dell'occupazione (massimo 1 anno)

Si lo ha hecho, ¿dónde y para quién?
Wenn ja, geben Sie den Ort und Namen des damaligen Arbeitgebers an
Si la réponse est positive, ou et pour le compte de qui?
Il the answer is yes, indicate: place of employment and Name of employer
In caso affermativo, indicare luogo e datore di lavoro

¿Ha trabajado otra vez en España?	Sí ☐	No ☐
Haben Sie vorher schon einmal in Spanien gearbeitet?	Ja ☐	Nein ☐
Avez-vous déjà travaillé en Espagne?	Oui ☐	Non ☐
Have you ever worked in Spain?	Yes ☐	No ☐
Ha gia lavorato in Spagna?	Si ☐	No ☐

Lugar y fecha / Ort und Datum / Lieu et date /
Place and date / Luogo e data

Firma del practicante / Die Unterschrift des Praktikanten /
Signature du stagiaire / Signature of applicant / Firma dell'interessarto

Amtlicher Zweck
Bitte sender Sie diesen Antrag auf Arbeitserlaubnis und Aufenthalts-oder Wohnsitzgenehmigung an:

Usage officiel
Transmettre cette demande de permis de travail et de séjour ou de residence temporaire a:

For official use
This application for a work permit and for a temporary and permanent residence permit to be sent to:

Uso Ufficiale
Inoltrare la presente richiesta di permesso di lavoro e soggiorno o residenza a:

Dirección General del Instituto Español de Emigración / Paseo del Pintor Rosales, 44-46 / 28008 MADRID (España)

Der Kandidat erfüllt die Bedingungen des Abkommens über

Le candidat remplit les conditions requises prevues par

The candidate complies with the conditions specified in the

Il candidato ha i requisiti previsti dall'accordo di intercam

torite competente du pays
d'origine

the competent authority of the
country of origin

rità competente del paese di
origine

Documentación unida / Beigefugte unterlagen / Documents joints / Documents attached / Documentazione allegata

Fotocopia del pasaporte en vigor, compulsada por un organismo oficial, y cuatro fotografías carné.
Beglaubigte Fotokopie des gültigen Passes und 4 Paßfotos.
Photo-copie du passeport en cours de validité, certifiée conforme par l'organisme officiel, et quatre photographies d'identité.
Photocopy of valid passport, certified by the relevant authority, and four passport-size photographs.
Fotocopia del passaporto non scaduto, autenticata dall'organismo ufficiale, e 4 fotografie formato tessera.

Duplicado de la solicitud de visado para trabajar presentada en el Consulado de origen.
Duplikat des beim zuständigen Konsulat vorgelegten Visumantrages auf Arbeit.
Duplicata de la demande de Visa pour travailler, présentée auprés du consulat d'origine.
Copy of the application for a work permit submitted to the Consulate of origin.
Copia della richiesta di visto per lavoro presentata presso il consolato di origine.

Certificado negativo de antecedentes penales del país de origen.
Führungszeugnis des Herkunftslandes ohne Eintragung.
Certificat de casier judiciaire vierge du pays d'origine.
Certificate indicating no criminal record issued by the country of origin (Letter of reference for U.K. Nationals).
Certificato penale rilasciato dal paese di origine.

Certificado médico del país de origen, negativo de enfermedades infectocontagiosas.
Ärztliches Attest aus dem Herkunftsland, daß keine ansteckenden Krankheiten vorliegen.
Certificat médical du pays d'origine, attestant que l'interessé ne souffre pas de maladies contagieuses.
Medical certificate from the country of origin stating that the applicant is free from any contagious disease.
Certificato medico rilasciato dal paese di origine, da cui risulti che d'interessato non e affetto da malattie infettive e/o contagiose.

Copia de diplomas y certificados de estudios.
Kopie des Ausbildungszeugnisses und Schulzeugnisse.
Copie du diplome et des certificats d'études.
Copies of educational qualifications.
Copia del diploma e titoli di studio.

Contrato de trabajo u oferta de empleo en prácticas.
Arbeitsvertrag und Praktikumsangebot.
Contrat de travail ou offre d'emploi comme stagiaire.
Work contract or valid offer for a training position.
Contratto di lavoro o offerta di formazione lavoro.

Resoluc.	TRABAJO APROBADO ☐ DENEGADO ☐
	FECHA CONCESION ⌐_⌐
	RESUELTO POR D PROV. ⌐_⌐ D. GRAL. ⌐_⌐
Resolución	RESIDENCIA ☐ APROBADA ☐ DENEGADA ☐
	ESTANCIA ☐
	FECHA DE CONCESION ⌐_⌐
	FECHA INICIO EFECTOS ⌐_⌐
	FECHA CADUCIDAD ⌐_⌐
	Nº DOCUMENTO ⌐_⌐

SPAIN

Imprimerie S.I.P.F. - Tél. : 46 54 27 07
N° d'impression 011 301
Dépôt légal 1er trimestre 1992